# School-to-Home
# CONNECTIONS
## Simple Strategies for Early Childhood Educators

### Cathryn O'Sullivan, EdM

**Gryphon** House
www.gryphonhouse.com

# Copyright

# Bulk Purchase

# Disclaimer

# Table of Contents

Dedication and Acknowledgments ................................................................. v

Welcome ................................................................................................... vi

Introduction ............................................................................................... 1

**Chapter 1:**
Put Your Oxygen Mask on First: The Importance of Self-Care ............... 3

**Chapter 2:**
Partnering with Parents ............................................................................. 9

**Chapter 3:**
Understanding the Power of Play .............................................................. 13

**Chapter 4:**
Intentional Interactions and the Power of *Yet* ........................................ 21

**Chapter 5:**
Involving Infants ...................................................................................... 27

**Chapter 6:**
Terrific Toddlers ...................................................................................... 35

**Chapter 7:**
Creating a Child-Centered Environment Where Children Thrive ........ 41

**Chapter 8:**
Setting up Child-Friendly Spaces ............................................................ 48

**Chapter 9:**
Building Child-Friendly Schedules .......................................................... 56

**Chapter 10:**
Encouraging Children's Individuality and Uniqueness ......................... 61

**Chapter 11:**
Embracing and Celebrating Our Diverse and Beautiful World ............. 66

**Chapter 12:**

Supporting Social-Emotional Development .......................................72

**Chapter 13:**

Language and Literacy ................................................................. 80

**Chapter 14:**

Fine-Motor Development and Writing ...................................... 88

**Chapter 15:**

Physical Development.................................................................. 96

**Chapter 16:**

STEM for Young Children ........................................................ 102

**Chapter 17:**

Nurturing in Nature..................................................................107

**Chapter 18:**

Behavior Is Communication ..................................................112

**Chapter 19:**

How Can I Tell If They're Learning?.......................................122

**Chapter 20:**

Handling Difficult Situations and Topics with Care................129

**Chapter 21:**

Transitioning to a New Class or School..................................136

Appendix: Children's Books Related to Different Topics .....................140

References and Recommended Reading ...........................................150

Index ............................................................................................159

## Dedication

Lovingly dedicated to Dr. Rose Davies. Thank you for all you did for early childhood development in Jamaica, and for me.

## Acknowledgments

I have been blessed with so much love and support throughout my life, and I am truly grateful. Thank you to my family and to my friends, who are the family I've been lucky enough to choose. Thank you to all of the educational and inspirational voices in my head and in my heart. I'll always try to keep listening to and learning from you.

Thank you to the children, families, teachers, and colleagues who have welcomed me and shared moments with me that have influenced and impacted me deeply.

Thank you to everyone who has contributed to this amazing opportunity. I hope I've made you proud.

Finally, thank you, readers, for choosing this book. I hope I can provide you with some support and encouragement, just as others have done for me.

# Welcome

Dear Teacher,

As a harried principal trying to get a brand-new preschool off the ground in my home country, Jamaica, I had become so inundated in daily chores, emergencies, and necessities that I'd lost the magic of the everyday, the magic of why we do what we do. You know that feeling—the one you get when you see a child smile as you approach, when they reach for your hand to help them toddle away from their parents. It's the joy you feel when you help a child practice walking around and around as their confidence grows, the magic of hearing a nonverbal child with autism repeat something you said or start singing when that child thinks no one is watching.

Jamaica—like many places—is a country that espouses the term *play based* while still trying to fully understand and embrace the concept. I was trying to introduce my teachers, who have decades of experience and a real and deep love for children, to a new, play-based, child-centered approach to seeing children and their roles in children's lives. I have scrambled to find the right training material: one that isn't too pedantic, that has just the right amount and type of tangible information teachers can digest and apply while on the job, that goes back to the basics while helping them to see that the foundation of a play-based teaching and learning process is magic. I hoped my teachers would understand that their role is to be intentional facilitators of magic for the children, which can only come from teachers enjoying and embracing each moment themselves. To do this, teachers need the knowledge, skills, and dispositions necessary to infuse every moment with intentional, playful foundational gems for children.

Our needs and roles as teachers have become even more apparent during the COVID-19 pandemic. We must not only consider our relationship with young children and how we maintain that connection (even when we can't see them in person) but also examine our relationship with the parents and help them to parent more effectively. We have to help them to manage full-day, well-rounded experiences with their children, and we have to figure out how to translate our knowledge and approach in a manner that they can digest and apply without feeling overwhelmed. Just a few little tweaks here and there can make a world of difference for us and for parents. This can only happen if we go back to the basics of what, how, and why we do what we do, so we can distill and condense this information to help us to keep going and to encourage and share with the parents.

Before the days got mired in deliverables and deadlines, what were your magical moments? What makes you smile and say, "This is why I'm here. This is why I keep going"? I hope this book not only helps you to hold on to those moments but also helps you to share easy suggestions so that parents, too, can have those magical moments with their children, so you all can help children to thrive.

Thank you for all that you do and all that you are.

With much love,

Aunty Cathryn

# Introduction

This book covers a range of subjects and areas relevant to your work with young children and their families. Each chapter addresses the challenges we educators face and offers suggestions for handling those challenges and communicating clearly with families. This book isn't meant to cover each topic exhaustively but to spark your interest, provide a few reminders and thought-provoking questions, or introduce new areas and ideas. At the core is my desire to remind you and the parents to let the children lead you; if you do, you won't go wrong. If you stay true to children's unique personalities, needs, abilities, and interests, then you'll always be on the right path.

## How to Use This Book

These (very short, I promise) chapters can be read straight through or in any order. You can choose the chapters you're most interested in, as each can stand alone, to provide you with quick tips for your environment. This book can also form the foundation for teacher professional development and conversation starters for professional-learning circles or informal conversations with your peers. A note about terminology: I know that many of us use different terms to describe ourselves and our profession, such as *practitioners, educators, caregivers, facilitators, teachers,* or *aunts/uncles*. For simplicity's sake, I will use the term *teacher*. I will also use the term *parent* to refer to children's main caregivers, guardians, or parents.

Use this book as a resource not only for you but also for parents, as you share the information with them so they can have guidance and suggestions for deepening their understanding of their children and supporting their learning and development. With each chapter, I've included a sample letter for parents addressing the topic of that chapter. The letters include information, resources, and ideas for connecting with parents, engaging them with the school community, and supporting them in their very important task of raising of a family. You can incorporate the text into your regular family communications or photocopy the letters and hand them out, sharing information on the topics of your choice.

If you'd like to dive deeper and learn more about a particular subject area, suggestions for additional reading are included at the end of most chapters. Websites such as Virtual Lab School (https://www.virtuallabschool.org/), Cox Campus (https://www.coxcampus.org/), Reading Rockets (https://www.readingrockets.org/), and the Center on the Social and Emotional Foundations for Early Learning (http://csefel.vanderbilt.edu/index.html) also offer resources and free, short online courses on a range of different topics for early childhood educators. The book also includes an appendix on pages 140-149 with a list of children's books related to the topics covered.

Go ahead, put your feet up, sip something soothing, and choose a topic that speaks to you. I hope that these pages will remind you that you are a superhero with the most awesome job in the world!

# Chapter 1:
## Put Your Oxygen Mask on First: The Importance of Self-Care

As teachers, we naturally give so much of ourselves to the children, their parents, and our colleagues that it's all too common for us to forget to take care of ourselves. We tend to forget the most important lesson: If we don't take care of ourselves, then we can't take care of anyone else. If we are depleting our tanks, then there will be nothing left to give, not only at school but also at home. We can't keep saying, "If I push on for just one more week/semester/year, I can _____ (insert goal or wish here). I just need to get through this _____ (insert far-fetched excuse here)."

Teacher burnout is a very real thing, and it's hard to put Humpty-Dumpty back together again once you fall off the wall. I worked so hard and squeezed myself through every tight space to get our preschool open. I was at the school for eleven hours every day for more than a year. The teachers and I learned to patch and paint walls. We used our own money to purchase supplies, sometimes without asking for reimbursement. (Does any of this sound familiar?) But then, I just couldn't do it anymore. I was too burned out. There was no more steam for the little engine who just couldn't.

In many ways, we teachers are actors. No matter what is happening inside, we do our best to always show and give children only our best. We hold everything in and keep going. But we have to find ways to care for ourselves every day, so that we can keep giving children our best. If you're honest with yourself, you'll recognize that when you're tired, sad, preoccupied, or worried, you aren't able to give your all. You're not able to be as consistent as you'd like with routines, encouragement, play, smiles, and behavior management strategies. That's completely understandable and human. The COVID-19 pandemic made it even more obvious how important personal interactions and relationships are, and those can't be forged if you're not caring for yourself.

Addressing burnout is particularly important because research has shown that teachers who experience a great deal of stress and feel burned out are not as likely to consistently create positive classroom climates and utilize effective classroom management strategies (Jeon et al. 2019; Shaack, Le, and Stedron 2020). They are also less emotionally connected and sensitive to children's needs and spend less time instructing children and communicating with families. Unsurprisingly, children in classrooms with burned-out teachers display more behavioral challenges and perform worse academically. This can then lead to teachers leaving the profession. In the United States, about 30 percent of early childhood teachers leave their jobs annually, which is four times higher than their counterparts in elementary school (Jeon et al. 2019; Shaack, Le, and Stedron 2020). Research tells us that self-care that addresses fatigue and stress may help to alleviate their effects (Cooklin, Giallo, and Rose 2011).

Self-care isn't selfish. It doesn't mean ignoring others or putting a wall up between yourself and those in your care. It does mean finding ways to take minibreaks, even just taking three deep belly breaths. It means getting the rest you need, seeking support from colleagues or mental health professionals before you are at a breaking point, asking for help, finding ways to disconnect from work and reconnect with yourself, and doing what you need to do to have a life you love to live.

## Breathe Deeply and Get Moving

When you need to center yourself and regroup, take at least three deep belly breaths where your belly gets bigger as you breathe in and deflates as you exhale. Try to make your exhale longer than your inhale. Practice this with the children in your class too! The earlier they start, the more of a lifelong habit deep breathing will become.

Even if you don't like regular exercise, you can find other ways to get moving. Movement is guaranteed to help you feel better. Go ahead! Make silly sounds, dance, move, shake, scream, and shake those negative emotions right out! You can even have movement and dance breaks in your learning environment. Are the children fidgeting and finding it hard to focus during story time? Stretch, dance, move, and breathe together, and then shift to calmer, slower movements as you settle back down.

## Laugh!

Laughter gives us so many benefits! It has been shown to positively affect our health and help us to live longer. It helps us to burn calories and tone muscles. Laughter helps the memory, helps prevent heart disease, and lowers the levels of the stress hormone cortisol. Laughter improves the mood. Even when nothing's funny, just choosing to laugh can have the same physical and emotional benefits as spontaneous laughter (Beasley 2020). Go ahead—try it alone and with the children.

## Find Gratitude and Support

Even when everything seems to be going wrong, pause, smile, and think about what you're grateful for. You can start a list together with the children in your class. You can make a gratitude corner where you and the children can place sticky notes of what you're grateful for. Keep a notebook of things that made you smile and feel grateful for during your day: the funny thing a child said, the a-ha moment a child had— you name it. Then, pick a random page and relive a moment whenever you need to!

Have a mini-support group you can talk with when you need a little help. You can take turns babysitting each other's children at home or supervising the children at school for a few minutes so you can take a longer break. You can just send each other words of encouragement and random memes that make you laugh! Don't be afraid to talk with a counselor or therapist if you need additional support for your mental health.

## Support Parents

Parents also get lost in their role, particularly parents with young children who require so much care, attention, and supervision. They too can forget to take care of themselves. As teachers, our role is to support parents in all aspects of parenting, not just the side we see when the children are with us. Sharing suggestions for their own self-care and reassuring them that taking time for themselves will help them to be better parents will not only be a welcome relief for them but also make your job easier as well.

Even a few tidbits here and there can brighten a parent's day. In the parent newsletter or email updates, include some of the funny things children say and do. Share funny or uplifting memes about parenting. Post encouraging signs. Provide opportunities for parents to get to know each other and talk together. At my old preschool, Sports Day, which was held outside, was the first school event that families were able to attend during the pandemic. After a year and a half of not getting to interact and share with each other, parents were so happy to mingle safely. It reminded us of how much fun they had had at the post–school concert parent potluck that was held before the pandemic.

No matter how you find time for yourself, just make sure to find the time. You simply can't take care of others if you aren't taking care of yourself!

If you'd like to explore more ideas, here's some additional reading about self-care:

Bethune, Adrian, and Emma Kell. 2021. *A Little Guide for Teachers: Teacher Wellbeing and Self-Care.* Thousand Oaks, CA: Corwin.

Boogren, Tina H. 2019. *180 Days of Self-Care for Busy Educators (A 36-Week Plan of Low-Cost Self-Care for Teachers and Educators).* Bloomington, IN: Solution Tree Press.

Forst, Sarah. 2020. *The Teacher's Guide to Self-Care: Build Resilience, Avoid Burnout, and Bring a Happier and Healthier You to the Classroom.* Evanston, IL: The Designer Teacher.

Dear Family,

It's okay to admit that you sometimes feel overwhelmed and exhausted. Every parent does—it means you're doing your job. It's also crucial that you admit that self-care isn't selfish. Feel free to say it out loud to yourself as many times and as boldly as you need to. **Self-care isn't selfish.** There's a reason you're told to put your oxygen mask on first before assisting others on a plane. You can't help anyone if you're struggling to breathe; you can only help when you are breathing freely. Tiredness and fatigue can negatively affect your physical and cognitive functioning and your interactions with your children, making you less patient and more frustrated and irritable. Research tells us that self-care that addresses this fatigue and stress may help to alleviate these effects.

Don't wait until you need a full-on escape (and won't want to come back). Instead, create a life you don't need to escape from. Try these quick and easy tips to slip some ease and "me time" into your packed days.

- **Breathe.** Take at least three deep belly breaths, where your belly gets bigger as you breathe in and deflates as you exhale. Try to make your exhale longer than your inhale. When your children see you breathing, they will also learn to try this too. The earlier they start, the more of a lifelong habit it will become. Rolling your eyes right now? Give it a try! What have you got to lose? Three deep breaths can make more of a difference than you think!

- **Take minibreaks.** Find little ways to take minibreaks throughout the day. If you struggle to supervise your little ones and need to take a break, use simple, tangible ways for them to understand. Sit nearby and give them something to play with independently. Then set a timer they can see for 5–15 minutes. Tell them that you're going to sit quietly, sip your tea, read a book, or look out the window and then you'll come play with them, they can come talk with you, and so on when the timer goes off. You can also say you'll join them after you finish playing two songs or you've finished eating or drinking something.

- **Get moving!** Even if you don't like regular exercise, you can find other ways to get moving. Movement is guaranteed to help you feel better. Go ahead! Make silly sounds, dance, move, shake, and scream those negative emotions right out!

- **Use routines as breaks too.** Turn routines and errands into more pleasurable experiences with simple swaps and shifts in thinking. During your child's bathtime, use soothing scents such as lavender to calm both you and your child. A whiff of some lavender-scented bubbles when you're washing the dishes wouldn't hurt either. Turn on your favorite songs or podcasts, and pause to notice how the warm water feels on your hands while you breathe in the scent.

▸ **Laugh!** Laughter has been shown to positively affect your health and help you to live longer. It helps you to burn calories, tones muscles, helps your memory, helps prevent heart disease, lowers levels of the stress hormone cortisol, and improves your mood, just to name a few benefits. Research tells us that even when nothing's funny, just choosing to laugh can have the same physical and emotional benefits as spontaneous laughter. Go ahead! Try it! What have you got to lose?

▸ **Think of things you're grateful for.** Even when everything seems to be going wrong, pause, smile, and think about what you're grateful for. You and your child can even list these things together. Keep a notebook of what has made you smile. What lovely, funny, spontaneous moment happened today? Collect these memories, and then pick a random page and relive a moment whenever you need to!

▸ **Get support.** Have a mini-support group you can talk with when you need a little help, or join a parenting group. You can take turns watching each other's children so you can take a longer break, or just send each other random memes that make you laugh!

Here are some books you can check out if you'd like to learn more ideas about self-care and parenting:

Costello, Judith, and Jurgen Haven. 2004. *Zen Parenting: The Art of Learning What You Already Know.* Silver Spring, MD: Gryphon House.

Dowling, Daisy, et al. 2021. *Taking Care of Yourself.* HBR Working Parents Series. Cambridge, MA: Harvard Business Review Press.

Pollak, Susan M. 2019. *Self-Compassion for Parents: Nurture Your Child by Caring for Yourself.* New York: Guilford Press.

Thank you for being our partner as we work together to nurture your incredible family. We're here to help and support you along the way. But don't worry—you've got this!

With warm and bright thoughts,

# Chapter 2:
## Partnering with Parents

The need to develop strong relationships with parents, caregivers, and families has never been more obvious than it was in 2020, as everyone struggled to support most young children who were suddenly told they could not come to school. Parents scrambled to figure out how to work from home and become instant teachers. Young children in particular are a challenging group to teach because they find online learning very difficult, if not impossible. They need hands-on experiences to meet their need for personal connection and exploration.

One of the most important messages you can share with parents at any time is to play with their children and allow their children to play. Everything comes from play, and parents need that reassurance and guidance now more than ever. Many parents will recall their own schooling experiences, which might have been very academic in nature. In Jamaica, most parents expect children to be able to write from a very early age. Parents use writing and homework assignments as a gauge for what children do all day and whether they are learning. Often, they do not understand that play is the best way to lay the foundation for later academic and personal success.

Home learning activities have a strong impact on children's readiness for kindergarten, regardless of children's socioeconomic background. The way early childhood teachers engage parents can have an indirect effect on children's school readiness through parents' home-based behavior and activities (Barnett et al. 2020; Kingston et al. 2013). A home-school partnership, therefore, is important in helping young children thrive.

If we start with the assumption that everyone is doing the best they can, then we can be more empathetic, even when we sometimes want to scream in frustration. In addition to the book's handouts and activity suggestions, you can support parents in understanding their role in helping their children to thrive.

## Parent Night

Inviting parents to participate at school by volunteering to read stories or share their skills, hobbies, cultures, and interests is, of course, a great way to encourage involvement. However, not all parents can take time during the school day to volunteer. You can go further by scheduling parent-night activities (virtual or in person) to encourage their connections with the school community and with each other. Don't have a big budget? Have a potluck so parents can also share a little bit of themselves and their culture with others.

### Play-Based Learning

To help parents understand the need for play-based, developmentally appropriate learning, plan a parent night. Offer play-based activities for the parents, such as the following:

▶ Have them create with playdough, so they can feel their fingers working and getting strong like their children's as the children prepare for writing.

▶ Invite them to play games, such as board games or hopscotch, so they can practice turn-taking and encouraging their peers.

▶ Provide animals, such as fish, frogs, turtles, or insects in tanks, for them to observe, so they can talk with their children about the different animals they see in their habitats. (Be sure to put the animals back where you found them, if you're not planning on keeping them in the classroom.)

▶ Provide art materials for open-ended exploration.

You can even do the same activity twice, once using hands-on, participant-centered methods and the other using more traditional, teacher-directed methods. Encourage parents to reflect on these experiences and discuss how they feel when they engage in each approach. They can even draw and color about their feelings before sharing. Open up a discussion about the ways they enjoy learning as adults, and compare that with the ways children learn. (They're probably quite similar.) They can also share their favorite memories of preschool and early learning experiences, which will probably involve play, connections, and developing strong relationships with their peers and teachers.

## Parent Mixers

Have parent mixers and events so they can get to know each other and make friends. Many parents, especially new or single parents, lack a support group of people who can empathize with their experiences, questions, joys, and concerns. Find out about parents' needs, interests, and areas of expertise so that you can incorporate these into your events. This approach will make the mixers more relevant and appealing to parents. You can hold a mixer virtually and invite parents to play fun games, chat, and share their talents with others. For example, invite a parent who is a yoga teacher to lead a short class, or invite a person who works at a supermarket to discuss budget-friendly meal planning.

This might all seem like more work for you, but having strong connections with parents helps them to become your partners as you work together to nurture and support children. Think about it: You don't want to hear only bad news or criticisms from your supervisors, but hearing criticism from someone you have a relationship with makes it easier to digest. Parents want and deserve a more rounded relationship with you. When parents understand your approach to teaching and learning and other areas such as discipline, they're less likely to complain about a practice. They're also more likely to give you the benefit of the doubt when an issue arises and to be more willing to listen to you if their child requires additional support.

Want to read more about building relationships with parents? Here's some suggested reading:

Ernst, Johnna D. 2014. *The Welcoming Classroom: Building Strong Home-to-School Connections for Early Learning.* Lewisville, NC: Gryphon House.

Kneipkamp, Janet R., and Robert E. Rockwell. 2003. *Partnering with Parents: Easy Programs to Involve Parents in the Early Learning Process.* Silver Spring, MD: Gryphon House.

Pepper, Alison. 2017. *Kick-Start Kindergarten Readiness.* Lewisville, NC: Gryphon House.

Dear Family,

Welcome to our family. We are excited to partner with you so that we can support your child's development and all grow together. We will be sharing tips and suggestions with you through handouts and family events, such as parent nights and workshops. We also look forward to getting to know you personally as we share with each other, so we can learn about your child's unique needs and approach to life and learning. Please feel free to reach out to us if you have any questions and suggestions or want to talk further, and we will do the same.

We will be sending out a list of our scheduled events soon. We hope that you will be able to join us!

Welcome again,

*School-to-Home Connections*   Gryphon House

# Chapter 3:
## Understanding the Power of Play

Most teachers have heard that young children learn best through play. We know, but do we really *know*? Have we fully understood and embraced what that really means? Have we considered the implications for this and infused it into our practices? In Jamaica, as we grapple with the conflicting demands of developmentally appropriate play-based practices and the overly academic demands to get children ready to move on to first grade, I've asked early childhood teachers if the children in their classes play. Most of the time the response is, "Yes, they play in the morning and in the afternoon, before and after school." The message here is that play isn't the base of the curriculum; it is a break from the curriculum. Play is fun, but surely children can't actually learn anything from it.

But they surely can! In fact, studies show that highly structured, scripted, primarily teacher-directed instruction is not as effective in promoting young children's academic success as is teaching that supports and extends children's self-initiated activities and interests (Bay Area Early Childhood Funders, 2007). Overuse of didactic or rote teaching can inhibit child-initiated learning and negatively impact young children's self-confidence and motivation to learn (Chang, Stipek, and Garza 2006; Shonkoff and Phillips 2000; Singer, Golinkoff, and Hirsh-Pasek 2006, as cited in Bay Area Early Childhood Funders 2007). Think about how you learn best, even as a grown-up. Do you like to laugh, try new things, engage with others, move and play? Or do you like to be told what to do and exactly how and when to do it?

You might face pressure from parents, supervisors, and teachers of older children who have developmentally inappropriate expectations of children. In Jamaica, many parents ask teachers of children as young as three, "What did my child write today? What is the homework?" Teachers feel pressured to live up to these expectations. This might be the only way that a parent knows how to gauge whether their child is learning, because this is how they grew up and were taught. If their children came home and pointed out interesting things they noticed on the walk, such as why leaves are green, or sang engaging songs as they did errands, they'd know their children were learning because they'd see and hear it in practice.

At the preschool I used to run, the mother of a three-year-old once said, "I wondered what my child did all day. I knew she was happy and playing, but I wondered what she was learning. Today we were talking about something, and she said, 'Well, it's hot in Jamaica because we are near the equator,' so now I know." When children are learning through play and learning is organic, their learning and growth will be obvious. Referencing standards as you plan your curriculum doesn't mean that you have to ignore play; they can go hand in hand as you set up your environment and plan for play with children's holistic development and developmental needs in mind (Jung and Jin 2014).

Play supports learning, researchers tell us (Ginsburg 2007, as cited in Dinkel and Snyder 2020; Bergen 2002, as cited in Bodrova and Leong 2003). So what does learning through play really mean? It means encouraging children to just be children and do what comes naturally and voluntarily: to play, to explore, to be, without an external goal (Neale 2020). It means noticing what they like and gravitate toward and including that to enhance their explorations. It means playing with them and having fun too. It means intentionally interacting with them and facilitating their interactions with you and their peers so they can become independent, critical thinkers and problem solvers. Here are some ways you can include more play throughout your day.

## Create Centers for Play

Set up centers for different types of play and exploration. Many, if not most, of you are probably rolling your eyes and saying, "Oh please, I've always had learning centers." But before you throw this book down in annoyance, pause and really think about what your vision and goal for the centers are, how you use them, and how the children use them. Free play is very different from "free-for-all play."

▶ Are you observing children and taking note of their interests so you can include prompts and materials in the centers and areas?

- ► Are you changing and tweaking the centers as necessary, based on children's interests and needs, to both support and stretch them?

- ► Are you really utilizing the centers throughout the day in a constructive way, or are they used as time fillers at times of the day when you need a break and don't really want to be involved?

Not sure? Invite an objective eye, such as a colleague, to observe during center time to see if they have any suggestions or insights. For those of you who use a more scripted or theme-based curriculum, include additional centers based on children's interests, wants, and needs.

## Make Time for Play

Do your schedule and activities allow for exploration and play? Do children have real ownership of their day, or do they play minimal, perfunctory roles based on what you think they can and should do? Whether you follow a more structured, scripted curriculum or an open-ended, emergent curriculum, you can always find ways to include play and playfulness. Following children's leads and interests won't detract from even the most scripted curriculum; instead, it can enhance it by allowing children to build on the things that keep them excited and engaged. Allow children to help you plan activities, and build time into your schedule so that you can follow their lead without feeling afraid you are going off script. Even introducing a new concept or teaching something new can be achieved through playful, hands-on methods. For example, to teach skip counting, lay out numbers on the floor and invite the children to skip the even numbers with you. I'd much rather skip over numbers laid out on the floor when learning about skip counting than memorize my two times table.

## Build on Children's Interests

Step back and observe the children, and jot down what you notice. What do they like playing with? What areas or activities don't get much attention? What kinds of conversations are they having? What kinds of group activities are they most engaged witht? least engaged with?

Plan authentic play experiences based on these observations, and continue to observe so that they can continue to grow. Cookie-cutter activities where everyone ends up with identical products are not very meaningful for children (and parents' refrigerators will do just fine without them). Encourage children to use open-ended materials, and the focus on the process and joy of creation and exploration will be far more beneficial. Even though the products on the refrigerators might be less polished than the cookie-cutter one, the children will be much prouder to display them.

## Play!

Play **with** them! Have fun too! If you're not having fun, they're not having fun. And if they're not having fun, they're not learning. Remember to really listen to and follow the children's lead, even if it sometimes seems to go against your bigger vision for play. Children might want to imitate older siblings and ask for homework or writing activities or sheets. How can you support their need to feel like "big kids" while honoring play? Perhaps they can do exciting activities at home with their families or have authentic writing opportunities, such as dictating questions for an adult to write before they interview a resource person or writing/drawing their observations on a clipboard during a field trip.

## Get Creative!

Children love to express themselves artistically—they love to sing, dance, draw, paint, move, act, and pretend. Let's face it, so do we (even if we might only admit to loving it when no one's watching). When I interviewed to be an assistant teacher at a preschool, they asked why I wanted to work with young children. Part of my answer was, "I love to sing, but I sing terribly. But young children don't know that, so I get to just sing."

I love the freedom we have to express ourselves without fear, to just give in to the joy, just like the children do. Children learn so much through the arts. Their cognitive, social-emotional, language, and physical skills are enhanced as they explore through open-ended experiences that support their creativity, imagination, efforts, and process, rather than making a product or producing a right answer (Mills 2014).

Music helps to strengthen both children's and adult's memories (Carlton 2000). You've probably noticed that children retain information learned through songs very quickly. At my school, one of the first times we heard the voice of one of our nonverbal children with autism was when he started singing and pointing to the letters we had up for "Bingo." We also noticed him doing the actions as we sang another popular song. As we sang songs such as "Old McDonald Had a Farm," we would wait for him to add "E I E I O" at the end. His chiming in at the end was an important building block for being able to engage in a conversation, similar to waiting for a turn to converse.

When you let go and share in the freedom that comes from play and creative exploration with children, you'll be surprised by not only how much joy it brings but also how many wonderful opportunities for growth and learning there are for all of you. Here's some suggested reading to help you harness the power of play and explore through the creative arts:

Bohart, Holly, Kathy Charner, and Derry Koralek, eds. 2015. *Exploring Play.* Spotlight on Young Children series. Washington, DC: National Association for the Education of Young Children.

Christakis, Erika. 2017. *The Importance of Being Little: What Young Children Really Need from Grownups.* New York: Penguin.

Connors, Abigail Flesch. 2004. *101 Rhythm Instrument Activities for Young Children.* Silver Spring, MD: Gryphon House.

Connors, Abigail Flesch. 2017. *Exploring the Science of Sounds: 100 Musical Activities for Young Children.* Lewisville, NC: Gryphon House.

Dinnerstein, Renée. 2016. *Choice Time: How to Deepen Learning through Inquiry and Play, PreK–2.* Portsmouth, NH: Heinemann.

Feldman, Jean, and Carolyn Kisloski. 2021. *The Possibilities of Play: Imaginative Learning Centers for Children Ages 3–6.* Lewisville, NC: Gryphon House.

Helm, Judy Harris. 2015. *Becoming Young Thinkers: Deep Project Work in the Classroom.* New York: Teachers College Press.

Jones, Elizabeth, and Gretchen Reynolds. 2011. *The Play's the Thing: Teachers' Roles in Children's Play.* 2nd ed. New York: Teachers College Press.

Kemple, Kristen M. 2017. *Planning for Play: Strategies for Guiding Preschool Learning.* Lewisville, NC: Gryphon House.

Kohl, MaryAnn F. 2000. *Big Messy Art.* Silver Spring, MD: Gryphon House.

Mraz, Kristine, Alison Porcelli, and Cheryl Tyler. 2016. *Purposeful Play: A Teacher's Guide to Igniting Deep and Joyful Learning across the Day.* Portsmouth, NH: Heinemann.

Patch, Casey. 2020. *Sensory Play for Toddlers and Preschoolers: Easy Projects to Develop Fine Motor Skills, Hand-Eye Coordination, and Early Measurement Concepts.* New York: Skyhorse Publishing.

Paterson, Anice, and David Wheway. 2021. *Kickstart Music: Music Activities Made Simple.* Rev. ed. Morrisville, NC: Lulu Press.

Pelo, Ann. 2016. *The Language of Art: Inquiry-Based Studio Practices in Early Childhood Settings.* 2nd ed. St. Paul, MN: Redleaf Press.

Silberg, Jackie. 1998. *The I Can't Sing Book for Grownups Who Can't Carry a Tune in a Paper Bag but Want to Do Music with Young Children.* Silver Spring, MD: Gryphon House.

Silberg, Jackie, and Pam Schiller. 2002. *The Complete Book of Rhymes, Songs, Poems, Fingerplays, and Chants.* Silver Spring, MD: Gryphon House.

Sluss, Dorothy Justus. 2014. *Supporting Play in Early Childhood: Environment, Curriculum, Assessment.* 3rd ed. Stamford, CT: Cengage.

Vanover, Sarah Taylor. 2020. *Building on Emergent Curriculum: The Power of Play for School Readiness.* Lewisville, NC: Gryphon House.

Zigler, Edward, Dorothy G. Singer, and Sandra J. Bishop-Josef. 2004. *Children's Play: The Roots of Reading.* Washington, DC: Zero to Three.

Dear Family,

I know it all sounds too good and too simple to be true, but it really is: Young children learn best through play. So just have fun! Your child's muddy messes are so much more than that! They're delicious new recipes, homes for plants and animals, and anything their imagination thinks they are. The box their present came in is always so much more exciting than the gift because they can decide what to do with it! A box can become a ship, a car, a snuggle cave and safe haven, a wall for drawings and writings, a basketball hoop, a hat—just about anything.

Play is critical for young children's development and promotes their cognitive, physical, social, and emotional well-being. Research tells us that play supports rather than detracts from their learning. Studies have shown that children in environments that nurture and build on children's self-initiated activities and interests do better academically than those in very structured, primarily teacher-directed environments, which can actually undermine their self-confidence and drive to learn.

Think back to your favorite childhood memories. What stands out? Go ahead and have fun with your children! No one will regret it.  Let them take the lead as you play together, and follow their ideas. You can even help their planning and comprehension skills by asking them to picture and describe what they'd like to do.

Use whatever you already have as props and toys. For example, empty paper-towel rolls make great building materials. You can even cut small slits around the top and bottom to act as notches so you can connect them. Schedule time (put it in your calendar if you have to) to make sure you have time to just play together.

Chores and errands don't have to feel like a chore. They can help you to cook and clean while you play little games like racing to see who can wipe the table the fastest or in the most creative way. You can play I Spy. Give clues such as "I spy something yellow," which can be anything yellow, or make it harder with more details: "I spy a yellow fruit." Make silly sounds, dance, and move while waiting in line. Ask your children to describe what they hear, smell, and see around them. Let them suggest games too!

Create a space for independent play. Make a play space together where your children can play safely and independently while you supervise, and play together when you can. They can decorate simple boxes for easy toy cleanup, place a sheet over two chairs to make a cozy fort, and choose their favorite books for their library box.

Get moving. Even just a short wiggle, stretch, and move break can help us feel more joyful. When everyone needs a quick pick-me-up, get moving! Dance to your favorite songs, wiggle, make silly poses, and sing silly songs if you don't have music. Enjoy!

Here are some books with suggestions for even more fun:

Featherstone, Phill, and Sally Featherstone. 2013. *50 Fantastic Things to Do with Preschoolers.* Lewisville, NC: Gryphon House.

Green, Rebecca. 2016. *Banish Boredom: Activities to Do with Kids That You'll Actually Enjoy.* Lewisville, NC: Gryphon House.

MacGregor, Cynthia. 2001. *Good Clean Fun: Over 70 Seriously Fun Games for Creative Families.* Silver Spring, MD: Gryphon House.

Playfully,

*School-to-Home Connections*   **Gryphon** House

# Chapter 4:
## Intentional Interactions and the Power of *Yet*

As you probably already know, you and your interactions and relationships with the children are the most important aspects of a high-quality program that helps children to thrive. According to the National Association for the Education of Young Children (NAEYC), two of the most important components of high-quality programs are teachers' interactions with children and a child-centered approach to learning. In its 2009 position paper on developmentally appropriate practice, NAEYC notes, "It is the teacher's classroom plans and organization, sensitivity and responsiveness to all the children, and moment-to-moment interactions with them that have the greatest impact on children's development and learning" (NAEYC 2009). Moreover, quality teacher-child interactions result in better cognitive, behavioral, and social outcomes (Mashburn et al. 2008). Even small differences in teacher-child interactions result in significant differences in children's outcomes (Howes et al. 2008). You really are the key. Even if that seems like quite a weight to carry, remember that your key unlocks children's potential just by following their lead and letting them play while you interact and play with them from this joyful place.

Teacher-child interactions affect outcomes by increasing children's engagement in learning. Effective teachers keep children engaged and nurture their ability to "learn to learn" by helping them develop their skills related to attention, persistence, and resilience. More effective interactions lead to more positive and constructive engagement by children (Vitiello, Hadden, and Teachstone Policy Group 2014). This approach will also help children to enjoy thinking and develop the dispositions they need to be a good thinkers: inquisitiveness, open mindedness, skepticism, attention to detail, and imagination (Ritchart and Perkins 2008, as cited in Birbili 2013).

## Nurturing a Growth Mindset

In Jamaica, where I'm from, much of our schooling—even during preschool—focuses on right versus wrong answers. The schooling in

Jamaica focuses on academics and academic intelligence, and many of us link our value to our grades. Praise is tied to doing well and being the best, not necessarily to effort. As students in Jamaica move on to secondary school and beyond, many of those who found academics easy and got good grades flounder when met with challenges, because they don't know how to try, persevere, or handle failure. Those who struggled academically (or were made to think they did because learning didn't come easily) might think of themselves as not smart and might not have been encouraged to nurture and focus areas where they could excel, such as through the arts.

When our interactions and approach to teaching and learning focus on giving right answers rather than problem solving, we are limiting not only children's beliefs about themselves and their abilities but also their ability to become critical thinkers. Children with a fixed mindset believe their ability is set and they can't do much about it; those with a growth mindset think that hard work, help from others, and other strategies can help them to develop their abilities (Haimovitz and Dweck 2017).

Studies have shown that children who are praised for their intelligence after they achieved success eventually start choosing tasks that are less difficult and focus more on being successful. They are not as motivated to try or focus on the process of learning. They also find it difficult to handle disappointment because they have internalized the idea that intelligence is fixed and not based on effort (Dweck 2008a, 2008b, as cited by Bayat 2011). Studies have also shown that three- and five-year-olds who are praised for their intelligence are more likely to cheat than their peers who are praised for their achievements or not praised at all (Zhao et al. 2017, as cited in Zhao et al. 2019). Furthermore, five-year-old children who overhear other classmates being praised for being smart are also more likely to cheat (Zhao et al. 2019).

Praising children by tying the praise to how you feel ("When you color in the lines, it makes me happy") or praising them for things they have little or no control over ("You're so pretty" or "You're so smart") doesn't help children to develop intrinsic or internal motivation to keep trying. Instead, they learn to wait for validation from you and other external factors or to think that there's nothing they can do to elicit praise— they're either pretty or smart or they aren't.

However, when children's efforts are recognized with praise such as "You're working really hard and really trying," then children are more motivated and likely to choose tasks that support their learning. They attribute failure to effort rather than to innate or fixed intelligence and are more focused on the ability to learn and grow. Focusing on praising children authentically for their process and demonstrated effort rather than for their intelligence helps children to keep trying even when things are difficult (Dweck 2006, 2007, as cited in Bayat 2011).

Here are some ways to nurture children's growth mindsets and thinking skills through intentional interactions:

▸ **Provide authentic praise.** Praise children authentically for their effort. It might seem like it's far too early to worry about this with little ones, that they're too young to receive this messaging anyway. But when they hear "I know this is hard but keep trying" or "I notice you're really working hard on that," your littles will know that you're praising them for trying their best. Positive reinforcement can include noticing effort, encouragement, and being a role model who talks about things you've struggled with and how you kept trying. If a child says, "I can't do it," respond with "You can't do it *yet*."

▸ **Teach that it's okay to change your mind.** While we encourage effort, we also need to rethink the term *quitting* and the stigma attached to it. It's okay for children (and us) to try our best and approach things with the best intentions but then realize that they don't like something or that it's causing them a lot of stress. It's okay for children (and us) to choose to stop doing something that has started to become unhealthy. Observe the children and listen to what they're sharing with you about different aspects of their lives. Maybe they really do have an aversion to messy sensory play, and it's causing them great distress while their classmates are squealing with delight. Or maybe they really would be much happier playing the maracas than the triangle, even though they initially begged to play the triangle. Help children's parents to understand this by sharing children's passions, interests, and aversions during a family night, or send a simple note updating them about their child. Provide them with specific tips about how they can encourage their child to persevere when things are challenging while acknowledging when they don't like something.

▶ **Intentionally use specific vocabulary.** As you play with the children, think of ways to subtly and naturally make every word count. The children at my former preschool have grown to expect me to count while they jump on the trampoline. They join in as they get older and are more exposed to counting over time. Instead of saying, "I'll tie the lace on *this* shoe," I say, "Let me tie your *left* shoe." We tie their shoes so often that they'll start to learn left and right without even noticing.

▶ **Ask open-ended questions.** Asking children open-ended questions that don't have right or wrong answers, and requiring them to say more than one word in their answer, helps them to develop critical-thinking skills. Asking questions such as "How do you think ____ was feeling when that happened?" or "Why do you think the baking soda started fizzing when the vinegar was added?" elicits much more thinking, processing, and sharing than "What color is this?"

When you approach your time with children with intention and fun, you'll build strong relationships with them so they feel secure and content to explore and learn. Keep talking **with** them and encouraging them to keep trying and just watch as their world opens up!

Here's some suggested reading about this topic:

Dweck, Carol. 2017. *Mindset: Changing the Way You Think to Fulfil Your Potential*. Rev. ed.. New York: Little, Brown.

Epstein, Ann S. 2014. *The Intentional Teacher: Choosing the Best Strategies for Young Children's Learning*. Rev. ed. Washington, DC: NAEYC.

Stead, Julia, and Ruchi Sabharwal. 2019. *Learning without Fear: A Practical Toolkit for Developing Growth Mindset in the Early Years and Primary Classroom*. Carmarthen, Wales, UK: Crown House Publishing.

Dear Family,

Your little ones learn so much just from your interactions with them. As you play and talk together, you not only have a wonderful opportunity to learn more about each other and the world around you but also can help them develop resilience—the strength to handle life's challenges. You can empower your children to believe in themselves and their efforts so they can keep trying, even when things are difficult. Helping children understand how powerful the word *yet* is will empower them to keep trying. For example, if your child is struggling to learn to tie their shoes and declares, "I give up! I can't do it!" you can reply, "You can't do it *yet*. Keep trying! Let me help you learn how to do it."

This belief that they can do difficult things, a growth mindset, is important in facing challenging times. Children with a growth mindset are more likely to keep trying and stay motivated even when things are hard. When children are praised authentically for their efforts—"You've been trying really hard," "You shared with your friend," or "You've been working to learn how to ride your bike, and you did it!"—they begin to understand that with hard work, help from others, and other strategies they can develop their abilities. Positive reinforcement can also just be about noticing effort, encouraging them, and being a role model who talks about things you've struggled with and how you kept trying. Also, read books together about characters who keep trying, such as *The Little Engine That Could* by Watty Piper, *The Carrot Seed* by Ruth Krauss, *Can I Play Too?* by Mo Willems, *Matthew's Dream* by Leo Lionni, *Train Your Dragon to Do Hard Things* by Steve Herman, and *A Chair for My Mother* by Vera B. Williams.

Not surprisingly, having a growth mindset, rather than thinking intelligence is fixed, tends to lead to better academic performance, especially for those who face challenges. It also makes children less likely to cheat than those who are praised for their intelligence or just overhear others being praised for being "smart." Children who receive feedback based on the process of learning, such as "What could you have done differently?" or "Why do you think that happened?" are more likely to develop a growth mindset (Haimovitz and Dweck 2017). Personal criticism can also negatively impact children and how they view themselves and their abilities.

Help your child to become a critical thinker and problem solver by asking open-ended questions—ones that don't have one right answer and require more than one word to answer. For example, rather than asking, "Did you have a good day?" which can result in just a yes or no, say, "Tell me about your day." This open-ended invitation can lead to a great conversation, especially when you include follow-up questions such as "What did you do then?" "Why do you think he did that?" or "It's okay that didn't go as you thought it would. What did you learn from it?"

While we want children to keep trying, sometimes it's okay to realize that something isn't for us and to let it go. Quitting because you realize something isn't for you and you are unhappy isn't the same as quitting because you don't even want to try or something is hard (an important lesson even for us as grown-ups). Encourage your children to keep trying and help them to find ways to address challenges and frustrations, but observe and listen to them if they're really just unhappy and truly just don't like something they're trying. Maybe they'd rather thrive in a different extracurricular activity than the one you've always hoped they'd like.

Be intentional in your conversations with your children. Even the everyday moments are opportunities for learning. Infuse little nuggets of knowledge wherever you can. For example, when tying their shoes or playing with them, use specific language such as "Give me your left foot," or "Throw the red ball." Over time, children will learn left and right or colors just from your simple interactions.

Just keep playing and having fun with your children and you'll find lots of little moments to stimulate, engage, and encourage them as you both learn from your special time together.

Playfully,

# Chapter 5:
## Involving Infants

At the preschool I helped to open, we welcome children from three months through five years of age. As the new teachers and I were planning the feel for the school, activities, layout, and so on, we struggled the most with planning for the infants and in hiring appropriate staff who had experience stimulating (not just supervising) this age group. Most of us had taught three-year-old children and older, and we wondered what children one year old and under do all day. Will the teachers in that room be bored? I've also heard similar sentiments from teachers at other child-care centers who aren't sure what to do when placed with this age group. Years later, it's been amazing to watch these children grow and play and to see how much we've all learned from them. They've become one of my favorite age groups to work with.

Teacher-child interactions are one of, if not the most, important component of child care. These interactions have a major impact on children's learning and development. Infants especially do well when they have strong relationships with warm, attentive teachers who engage with them and respond to their needs and ways of communicating while supporting them as they explore (Chaudry and Sandstrom 2020). Children up to twelve months grow and change so quickly, and you can do lots of things to stimulate them and have fun at the same time.

## Observe and Plan

As with any age, when you start with the specific children's interests and needs as your foundation, you can't go wrong. Children don't need to be able to talk or complete a survey to tell you what they like. You can see it in their expressions and hear it in their squeals of delight and shrieks of disdain. You notice it in the types of toys and activities they gravitate toward. Jot down what you notice, and set up learning environments that support their interests, remembering that you might need to design different zones to accommodate different children's needs. For example, children who are learning to sit up will need much softer and thicker mats and flooring than those who are walking, so they can safely sit up and fall back down again without hurting themselves. Those who are practicing to pull up will benefit from a pull-up bar and safe shelving they can use for practice.

Once babies are awake, they should be out of their cribs and engaged or exploring their environment. If you share your space with rambunctious toddlers, you might need a small, safe, separated area away from the toddlers. The youngest babies will need an area where they can safely enjoy tummy time and explore objects without being hurt by children who are enjoying their new walking and running skills. You can do this by rearranging furniture or using a baby gate.

Talk with the children, even if they can't talk back yet. When you do, you're laying the foundation for language development and so much more. Your back-and-forth conversations as you respond to their coos will support social-emotional development too, as they realize that they can elicit a response to their cues and noises and that they can respond to you. They will also see that your response changes based on the emotion they are sharing. When you meet cries with soothing tones and smiles and meet giggles with laughter and happy tones, they will learn that you hear them and care about them. They can't get this type of interaction from a screen.

Infants in particular have many set routines in their day, such as multiple feeding and changing times. These are wonderful opportunities for individual interactions with real words (not made-up baby talk) so they can be exposed to lots of vocabulary from the very beginning (*The Guardian* 2020). Describe what you are doing as you are changing them. Sometimes fussy children who don't like being changed might prefer one of their favorite songs and engaging facial expressions to comfort them. Talk with your littles as you feed them: describe the food and how it tastes, and ask them if they like it while you encourage them to explore it with their hands and mouths.

This serve and return, like in a tennis match, helps children to learn that what they say matters and that a relevant and matched response will be made based on what they "said" and the emotions they shared through their expressions, tone, and body language.

## Stimulate with Simple Activities

There are many ways to stimulate little ones without breaking the bank. You just have to embrace your inner hoarder and remember that engaging infants is easy because you're introducing them to almost everything! Here are some examples of simple activities:

- ▸ **Sensory bottles:** Fill small plastic bottles with water, oil, food coloring, paper clips, and other small objects (and seal them tightly so little hands can't open them).

- ▸ **Shaky sounds:** Add pebbles, sticks, paper clips, and other small objects to empty plastic bottles (and seal them tightly so little hands can't open them). Babies can explore the different sounds made when they shake the bottles. These are also great instruments as they sing along with you.

- ▸ **Sensory baskets:** Create sensory baskets by adding strips of cloth and other items safe for them to touch, taste, smell, see, and hear.

- ▸ **Sensory hoops:** Wrap different textured items around a large plastic hoop, and place a baby in the middle during tummy time.

## Create Predictable Routines

While there will always be a beautiful unpredictability about a day with young children, children do best when they can follow predictable routines to help them understand what will happen during their day. In our school, even our youngest children started to understand and look forward to snack time, which followed circle time each morning. They would crawl and toddle over to their tables and chairs without being asked.

Adding a schedule with pictures will also help infants understand the day's progression. Young children's schedules should include lots of time for exploration and play, both inside and outside. Rest and feeding times will vary by their age and individual needs, particularly for the youngest infants.

Having a schedule doesn't mean that you don't allow for spontaneous events or extend time for activities that children are really enjoying. Nor does it mean that you're going to introduce activities that are far too academic and developmentally inappropriate. A schedule helps you to think of children's varying needs and interests and supports your planning as you consider different engaging activities, such as song and story times and small-group explorations. Because of their short attention spans, infants won't necessarily listen to the entire story or be interested in singing a lot of songs (though some might surprise you). Be mindful of their moods and level of focus, and adjust when you need to, cutting one activity short while extending another that they seem very engaged in.

As you watch the infants develop and change, you'll start to see indicators of what they've learned from their explorations and experiences with you. They'll start clapping and cooing along to their favorite songs and gravitate toward the activities and toys that interest them the most. As you interact and play with them, you'll find that engaging infants can be just as engaging for you too.

If parents need a little extra support in understanding how to engage with their children or you notice that they tend to have similar questions or concerns about infant development, hold a parenting workshop for them and invite a pediatrician or other resource person.

Here's some additional reading to help you care for your littlest ones:

Daly, Lisa, and Miriam Beloglovsky. 2016. *Loose Parts 2: Inspiring Play with Infants and Toddlers.* St. Paul, MN: Redleaf Press.

Da Ros-Voseles, Denise, and Beverly Kovach. 2008. *Being with Babies: Understanding and Responding to the Infants in Your Care.* Silver Spring, MD: Gryphon House.

Day, Monimalika, and Rebecca Parlakian. 2003. *How Culture Shapes Social-Emotional Development: Implications for Practice in Infant–Family Programs.* Washington, DC: Zero to Three.

Lewin-Benham, Ann. 2010. *Infants and Toddlers at Work: Using Reggio-Inspired Materials to Support Brain Development.* New York: Teachers College Press.

Miller, Linda G., and Kay Albrecht. 2000. *Innovations: The Comprehensive Infant Curriculum.* Silver Spring, MD: Gryphon House.

Miller, Linda G., and Kay Albrecht. 2001. *Innovations: A Self-Directed Teacher's Guide.* The Comprehensive Infant Curriculum series. Silver Spring, MD: Gryphon House.

Read, Amy B., and Saroj N. Ghoting. 2015. *Time for a Story: Sharing Books with Infants and Toddlers.* Lewisville, NC: Gryphon House.

Wilhelm, Laura. 2017. *Treasure Basket Explorations: Heuristic Learning for Infants and Toddlers.* Lewisville, NC: Gryphon House.

Wittmer, Donna, ed. 2017. *The Encyclopedia of Infant and Toddler Activities for Children Birth to 3.* Rev. ed. Lewisville, NC: Gryphon House.

Wittmer, Donna, and Deanna W. Clauson. 2018. *From Biting to Hugging: Understanding Social Development in Infants and Toddlers.* Lewisville, NC: Gryphon House.

Wittmer, Donna, and Deanna W. Clauson. 2020. *Crying and Laughing: The Emotional Development of Infants and Toddlers.* Lewisville, NC: Gryphon House.

Zero to Three. 2008. *Caring for Infants and Toddlers in Groups: Developmentally Appropriate Practice.* 2nd ed. Washington, DC: Zero to Three.

Dear Family,

You might be too sleep deprived to think about what else you can do to engage your infant, but hang in there. Here are a few easy ways you can stimulate your child. If you base your decisions on the premise that even babies want to be encouraged and loved as they try to be as independent as possible, then everything will flow from there.

Infants love to hear their special people talk. Point out things when you're driving, or just read your work emails out loud in a soothing tone during bedtime (reading a particularly annoying email in a silly voice might even help you feel less angry about it). It's never too early to starting talking with babies. When you use "parentese"—that natural, happy, singsong voice where you say words playfully in different pitches to speak with your baby using real words (not made-up baby talk)—you will help your child develop vocabulary. The back-and-forth exchange that happens when you talk to them—you talk, they coo and smile back, and you respond again—helps them develop important language and social-emotional skills.

Here are some examples of things you can do with your baby:

▶ **Talk, talk, talk.** Make routines fun! You and your little one have so many routines—changing, feeding, and bathing—that you can turn into magical moments for meaningful interactions. Talk with your baby, and describe what you're doing.

- Bathtime: "I'm giving you a bath! Let's put some soap on the washcloth. Next, I'll wash your little back and rinse it with this cool water. Wash, wash, wash, splash, splash, splash."

- Feeding: "Oh, you really like your carrots. I see you smiling! Yummy orange carrots!"

- When you get home: "I'm so happy to see you! We delivered a lot of orders today. We delivered an order to a business on Third Street, then another order to the hospital. We were so busy! But now I'm home with you! What did you do today? I see some red paint on your shirt. Did you do some painting?"

- Changing a diaper: "First, let's take off this dirty diaper. Then I'll use a wipe to clean you up. Next, I'll put on a little diaper cream. Does that feel better? Now, I'll put on a clean diaper."

- **Sing.** Singing songs while you're changing your baby might soothe a fussy child (and you); go ahead and add some silly faces to really make it fun for both of you. Sing while you're sitting outside in the fresh air. Sing while you're bathing your baby. Children don't care whether you can carry a tune; they just love to hear you sing.

- **Play, play, play!** Infants need time out of their crib to play and explore. You can set up a simple area near you where your baby can safely lie on the floor for tummy time. (Make sure there's padding if your child is practicing to sit up.) If your baby is crawling, put favorite objects nearby to encourage them to try to reach or crawl for the objects. You can make simple toys by placing colorful items such as paper clips in a small unbreakable bottle of water and then seal it with glue. Infants have tons of fun rolling and shaking the bottles. Put a little paint or hair gel and food coloring in a transparent resealable bag and seal it carefully with tape. Your baby can have fun squishing it and tapping it during tummy time.

- **Read with me!** Babies love hearing their parents' voices, and they're learning new words and all about our language at the same time. Read baby books with them, pointing to pictures and naming the words. Need to catch up on work emails and documents? Read them out loud to your little one, using funny voices and soothing tones, which might even help you to digest them better!

- **Let me try! Give me choices.** Are you subconsciously ignoring your baby's signs that they want to do things, such as holding their bottle by themselves because you're too nervous they can't do it and will make a mess or you want them to be your baby forever? Infants will start picking up on these cues and start learning that their parents can do it better than they can so they don't really need to try. This might be why you notice your baby doing more things and responding differently at child care than they do when they're with you. Support your baby as they try to do things by themselves. Facilitate their ability to make choices and make their preferences known by noticing their expressions and sounds. Do they change when they are around a certain toy or person or when they hear different sounds? Introduce new foods one at a time instead of blending them all together, so you can easily discern what they like from what they don't.

The most important thing to remember about parenting children at any age is that you are all they really need. You are their favorite toy! Just have fun together, and the rest will fall into place.

*School-to-Home Connections* **Gryphon** House

Here are a few book suggestions for further reading:

Borgenicht, Louis, and Joe Borgenicht. 2012. *The Baby Owner's Manual: Operating Instructions, Trouble-Shooting Tips, and Advice on First-Year Maintenance.* Philadelphia, PA: Quirk Books.

Davies, Simone, and Junnifa Uzodike. 2021. *The Montessori Baby: A Parent's Guide to Nurturing Your Baby with Love, Respect, and Understanding.* New York: Workman Publishing.

Marinovich, Ayelet. 2018. *Understanding Your Baby Birth to 12 Months: A Week-By-Week Development and Activity Guide for Playing with Your Baby.* Mountain View, CA: Strength in Words.

Murkoff, Heidi. 2014. *What to Expect the First Year.* 3rd ed. New York: Workman Publishing.

Warmly,

*School-to-Home Connections*  Gryphon House

# Chapter 6:
## Terrific Toddlers

Teaching toddlers can sometimes feel confusing. They're adding new words all the time and are more independent and inquisitive than infants but are not ready for more academic concepts, despite what their parents might think. So what do you do with them all day? How do you stimulate them without overwhelming them?

## Plan for Their Specific Needs and Interests

Like all children, toddlers will develop at different rates and require a wide variety of activities and materials. They're much more vocal about their preferences, and even if you don't understand their words, their babble's tone and facial expressions will tell you everything you need to know. Toddlers aren't developmentally ready to share yet and are slowly starting to show more interest in playing near, and possibly with, other children. If there are items that are particular favorites, include enough so they can all play with the same thing at the same time.

They're still exploring through all of their senses, so be sure to use materials that are not choking hazards and can be sanitized or replaced easily. Supplying enough safe materials doesn't have to break the bank:

- ▶ Dolls can be made from simple materials such as scraps of cloth.

- ▶ Easy blocks can be made with clean, dry sponges.

- ▶ Provide empty paper-towel rolls with slits cut at the top and bottom to make notches.

- ▶ Empty paper-towel rolls also make great ball drops with balls or balled-up socks.

- ▶ Balls and small, unbreakable bottles make a great bowling game.

- ▶ Kitchen utensils such as whisks, measuring cups and spoons, sieves, and colanders make great dramatic-play toys.

## Encourage Exploration

Toddlers still have very short attention spans and shouldn't be expected to sit and focus for more than a few minutes. You can still include some flexible, small- and whole-group fun into your schedule. The little ones can toddle in and out and participate as they choose. For example, they love expressing themselves creatively. Sing and dance with them throughout the day, and encourage them to dance freely and move around and include movements for songs that they'll enjoy copying. Have short story times and read throughout the day as they bring you books. Let them do simple experiments such as mixing baking soda, food coloring, and vinegar and playing around with the eruption. Spend lots of time exploring and playing freely while you facilitate and observe so you can plan more activities and decide on needed materials.

## Play Together

Describe what's happening while you play and talk together. Use self-talk to describe what you're doing, such as "I'm going to roll the blue playdough into a ball," and parallel talk to describe what they're doing, such as "I notice that you're collecting all these leaves and piling them up." Model how to extend sentences as you respond to them. If a child says, "Go up," you can say, "You want to climb up the ladder?"

At the preschool I used to run, our toddler teachers were amazed at how much the children could pick up just through consistent conversation and description. Over time, the children learned colors as teachers said sentences such as, "Wow! You got a blue ball. Now I'm going to pick a purple one." One of the teachers said to me, "You know, I'm so used to teaching everything with a chart and drilling colors and other concepts, but I can't believe how much they've picked up just while we're playing."

If you notice that children are picking up on the concepts you're introducing, such as counting while singing or counting how many times they jumped on the trampoline, it's okay to slowly introduce more academic concepts in an appropriate way. For example, count out loud as you put toys back in their basket, or point to letters as you sing a favorite letter song they might have learned at home. Remember, for this age everything is a learning experience, so don't take tasks that might seem simple for granted. Practicing self-help skills such as washing their hands independently, spooning things out, taking deep breaths to calm down when upset, waiting for their turn, and transitioning between activities are setting them up for later success in school.

## Offer Roles and Provide Routines

Toddlers love routines and being helpful "big kids." Post a visual schedule with pictures showing the day's activities, and reference it throughout the day to help children to understand what's coming next. Encourage them to have roles and responsibilities in their space by showing them how to clean up, push in their chair after eating, and help their peers.

Toddlers are excited to start spreading their wings and exploring independently. Just follow their lead, build on their interests, and share in their joy!

Here's some further reading about toddlers:

Albrecht, Kay, and Linda G. Miller. 2000. *Innovations: The Comprehensive Toddler Curriculum.* Silver Spring, MD: Gryphon House.

Buhr, Erin. 2018. *Little Walks, Big Adventures: 50+ Ideas for Exploring with Toddlers.* Lewisville, NC: Gryphon House.

Daly, Lisa, and Miriam Beloglovsky. 2016. *Loose Parts 2: Inspiring Play with Infants and Toddlers.* St. Paul, MN: Redleaf Press.

Lewin-Benham, Ann. 2010. *Infants and Toddlers at Work: Using Reggio-Inspired Materials to Support Brain Development.* New York: Teachers College Press.

Masterson, Marie. 2018. *Let's Talk Toddlers: A Practical Guide to High-Quality Teaching.* St. Paul, MN: Redleaf Press.

Miller, Karen. 1999. *Simple Steps: Developmental Activities for Infants, Toddlers, and Two-Year-Olds.* Silver Spring, MD: Gryphon House.

Read, Amy B., and Saroj N. Ghoting. 2015. *Time for a Story: Sharing Books with Infants and Toddlers.* Lewisville, NC: Gryphon House.

Schiller, Pam, and Thomas Moore. 2006. *And the Cow Jumped Over the Moon: Over 650 Activities to Teach Toddlers Using Familiar Rhymes and Songs.* Silver Spring, MD: Gryphon House.

Wilhelm, Laura. 2017. *Treasure Basket Explorations: Heuristic Learning for Infants and Toddlers.* Lewisville, NC: Gryphon House.

Wittmer, Donna, ed. 2017. *The Encyclopedia of Infant and Toddler Activities for Children Birth to 3.* Rev. ed. Lewisville, NC: Gryphon House.

Wittmer, Donna, and Deanna W. Clauson. 2018. *From Biting to Hugging: Understanding Social Development in Infants and Toddlers.* Lewisville, NC: Gryphon House.

Wittmer, Donna, and Deanna W. Clauson. 2020. *Crying and Laughing: The Emotional Development of Infants and Toddlers.* Lewisville, NC: Gryphon House.

Dear Family,

Are you wondering where the time went? It feels like your baby has suddenly turned into a moving, grooving, tantruming, talking toddler whose personality is shining right through (for better or for worse). You might be wondering how best to stimulate your child during this in-between time when they're old enough to do a lot more things independently but far too young to delve into more academic activities.

▶ **Play with them.** You may be tired of hearing this, but play really is the best thing you can do with, and for, young children as they grow. Let them play, explore, and lead you as you play together. Talk about what you are doing together, and talk with them. Ask questions, respond to their words and babbles, even if you aren't sure what they're saying, and just keep having fun together as you keep the back-and-forth conversation going. Extend what they're saying to help them make longer sentences. For example, if your child says, "Big dog," you can say, "Yes, that's a very big dog called a Doberman."

▶ **Describe the world around them.** Young children are little sponges soaking up everything around them and learning new vocabulary words even before they can say them. Don't be afraid to use "big" words around them. Every word is a new word, so you might as well introduce lots of them. Describe what you see around you, name new things as you read, and describe what you and they are doing. Saying, for example, "We are coloring with red crayons" or "I see you clapping your hands," will help build their language and vocabulary skills while subtly introducing important concepts such as colors.

▶ **Sing and dance together.** Most toddlers love singing and dancing and can learn to follow and repeat simple movements. As they start, stop, and wait for cues, children are developing important self-regulation skills. They're learning key vocabulary words from the songs too. Singing and dancing with you is much more effective than following along from a screen alone. You can respond to their cues, explain new words, and change your tone and moves to keep it fresh for them, which are important tools as they develop socially. It's okay to include counting and alphabet songs and to point to numbers and letters as you sing. Just don't drill your children to learn them before they're ready. A gentle introduction will lay the foundation for them when they're ready to learn during preschool.

- ▸ **Create "yes" environments.** Ever wonder why *no* is a toddler's favorite word? It's probably because it's the word they've heard most often from their parents and everyone around them. Toddlers are gaining more independence and want to do more things on their own. They want to explore through touch, taste, sight, sound, and smell—you name it, they want to know about it. Set up their environment so they can explore safely without hearing *no* and *don't* all the time. Look around your space and think about modifications you can make, such as covering the sockets and replacing breakable or special objects with other interesting items they can practice touching carefully. Remember, it's just as much their home as yours.

- ▸ **Guide them with simple explanations.** Newly independent, highly inquisitive toddlers are learning a lot right now and need guidance rather than reprimands for things they really don't know yet. Just saying *no* or *stop* doesn't tell children what to do or how to do it the next time. Give a short explanation, and show them what they can do instead. For example, showing them how to use gentle touches when playing with the puppy will help them understand not to pull its hair and won't make them feel bad for not knowing what to do. Redirect them to a safer, more engaging activity when possible.

As you spend more time having fun and interacting with your toddler, you'll realize that you can easily replace your fears of the "terrible twos" with the joys of the "terrific twos." Want to learn more? Here are some book suggestions:

Buhr, Erin. 2018. *Little Walks, Big Adventures: 50+ Ideas for Exploring with Toddlers*. Lewisville, NC: Gryphon House.

Lansbury, Janet. 2014. *No Bad Kids: Toddler Discipline without Shame*. Scotts Valley, CA: CreateSpace.

Warmly,

# Chapter 7:
## Creating a Child-Centered Environment Where Children Thrive

Your approach to the children you work with and the teaching and learning process is the most important component to support children's development. Studies have shown that *process quality*— the actual experiences children encounter such as teacher-child and peer interactions and the atmosphere in the learning environment—is a powerful predictor of children's development and learning. These experiences are even more powerful than the structural elements of a program's quality, such as teacher education, class size, and classroom materials (Vitiello, Hadden, and Teachstone Policy Group 2014).

Regardless of which curriculum you use and how you schedule your day with children, the most important thing you can do is to keep the children you serve at the forefront of whatever you're doing. Every decision, every plan, every consideration about layout, activities, assessments, goals, food—you name it—should be preceded by "What would my littles think? Would this work for them? Would they like this? What do they need?"

This can sometimes feel challenging when you're inundated with demands from supervisors, parents, school systems, and colleagues, but using the children as your compass will never steer you wrong. When competing voices distract you and seem to drown out those of the children, close your eyes, take a few deep breaths, and listen carefully. What are the children trying to tell you? What does your gut tell you is the right thing to do for them? What would you want if you were them? They have just as many rights, thoughts, wants, needs, and personalities as grown-ups do, just in smaller packages. When all of the other stakeholders see the light in the children's eyes, they'll know you made the right decision. They'll see that the children will be fired up and learning. Here are some tips to help you let children lead your approach and your environment, regardless of your center's philosophy.

## Start with Children's Interests

Observe children and listen to their conversations with peers to discover what they're interested and engaged in. Include those topics in your planning. If you use an emergent or Reggio-based curriculum, this might be the expectation. However, even if you use a theme-based curriculum, you don't have to feel restricted. You can always find ways to insert children's interests into your activities and learning centers. For example, you can do mini projects on specific areas of interest within the theme or create an extra center or interest area where children can explore this further. If you have a transportation theme, and children seem particularly fascinated with wheels, you could invite children to participate in the following:

- ▶ Investigate different types of wheels—their sizes, shape (what would happen if they made a square wheel?), and use.

- ▶ Explore how wheels help things to move and what would happen if there weren't wheels.

- ▶ Investigate friction, how wheels move on different surfaces, and where they can find wheels.  Explore different wheel tracks and make prints and patterns on surfaces such as sand, playdough, and paint.

## Find Ways You Can Involve Children More

Always ask, "How can I involve children more?" When you start with this question, you allow yourself to brainstorm the possibilities in every area. You will see your learning environment and approach to teaching and learning as flexible and ever changing as you partner with the little ones you care for. Think about the following through the lens of involving the children.

- ▶ Could children help with the simple chores you hate doing but they'd love to take ownership of? Young children love helping with grown-up chores such as sweeping and wiping and setting the table. Make changing the sand in the sensory table into a game for children instead of a tedious chore for you. Hide a few pieces of "treasure" for them to find as the table empties. As they're helping you to scoop up the sand, count how many little cups it takes to fill the big bucket. Have a race to see who can fill their bucket the fastest (while helping them to practice being careful so the sand doesn't fly around).

▶ Could they brainstorm and plan activities with you? For example, you could ask them to suggest things they'd like to learn more about or explore for an upcoming theme, or you can even brainstorm the theme together. They might have suggestions for the best way to clean up a mess or avoid it altogether. Children can also be great problem solvers, so ask them what they think you should do if a lot of children want to use the same center at the same time. Perhaps they'll suggest making one center larger and another smaller or taking turns by using a list and timer.

▶ What about the learning environment? Have you ever asked them where they think each center or item could go? Have you asked their ideas for what should be included in a center, such as adding new play food to make a different restaurant in dramatic play, or adding loose parts to make their own vehicles to drive around their construction site? Have you asked what they think of the seating arrangements and whether they'd sometimes prefer to color while sitting on the floor using a clipboard rather than sitting at the tables? Maybe they'd even like to sit together in larger or smaller groups or change who are they sitting beside to get to know other children.

▶ Are you having problems with scheduling because your children always take ages to settle down at rest time? What suggestions could they have for that? Perhaps they will ask for an extra story or a quiet-time song, or maybe they need a nightlight or lamp because they think the room is too dark.

Even nonverbal children and the youngest ones we serve have opinions, although they can't express them with words. Your observations can tell you a lot about whether a routine, activity, or layout is working well for them. Don't be afraid to just pause, step back, and notice. Asking children will also reveal more than you think. Let them lead you.

Do you say *yes* more than you say *no*? This is a very hard one, I know, especially because it's your job to keep children safe and to teach them about how to keep themselves safe. But if you're always saying no, are your environment and approach too restrictive and not inherently child friendly? If you constantly have to tell children what they can't do, how will they explore and learn what they *can* do?

Are there modifications or changes you can make to help the children explore freely and safely? For example, if they are always climbing on shelves and furniture, is there a simple and safe climbing tool you could purchase or have built that would meet this need? Perhaps they need more opportunities to move throughout the day. If you have too few toys or materials, making you too afraid to let children just play with them, then how can they learn and experiment? Can you add to the classroom toys and materials? For example, can you make items from recyclables or "trashables"? Think about what is holding you back from saying yes, and try to find a way to eliminate that barrier.

## Focus on What Children Can Do

Create the environment in a way that children can take as much ownership over it as possible. They can help you to prepare and serve snack, pour water whenever they'd like from small pitchers, access a child-sized broom when they need to clean up, and help their peers to get their shoes for outside play. Tangible tips, such as reminding them to listen for the click when closing markers or checking that they've turned off the lamp when they leave their cozy library center, go a long way toward empowering them and allowing you to relinquish much of the control.

"Focus on what children can do rather than what they can't." My friend Hilary runs a school for children with severe and multiple disabilities. Recently, she reminded me of this very important message that should be the core of all we do. When talking with prospective parents—who usually start by explaining what their child can't do to see if the school can support them—Hilary changes the conversation and says, "Tell me about what your child can do." She says that the parents' demeanors change instantly. They list all of the wonderful things their child can do, and they, in turn, start to see their child differently, as more capable and powerful than they had considered before. Their child, in turn, feels more capable and powerful.

When you approach children based on what they can do rather than what they can't, an entire world of possibilities opens up. You can build on these strengths and interests through your approach, environment, activities, and interactions, differentiating as necessary to meet each individual child's needs.

Here are some books to help you explore further:

Bruski, Nancy. 2013. *The Insightful Teacher: Reflective Strategies to Shape Your Early Childhood Classroom.* Lewisville, NC: Gryphon House.

Copple, Carol, and Sue Bredekamp. 2008. *Developmentally Appropriate Practice in Early Childhood Programs Serving Children from Birth through Age 8.* 3rd ed. Washington, DC: National Association for the Education of Young Children.

Curtis, Deb. 2017. *Really Seeing Children: A Collection of Teaching and Learning Stories.* Lincoln, NE: Exchange Press.

Feldman, Enrique. 2011. *Living Like a Child: Learn, Live, and Teach Creatively.* St. Paul, MN: Redleaf Press.

Gestwicki, Carol. 2016. *Developmentally Appropriate Practice: Curriculum and Development in Early Education.* 6th ed. Boston, MA: Cengage Learning.

Wurm, Julianne. 2005. *Working in the Reggio Way: A Beginner's Guide for American Teachers.* St. Paul, MN: Redleaf Press.

Dear Family,

There's no need to worry about whether you are enough for your children. You are all they need, and all they need from you is that you just let them be themselves. Give them the room, respect, and support to discover who that is. The way you see your children plays a huge role in how you parent and in how they see themselves and their abilities. If you see them as less capable or don't value what they say, then they'll stop trying, and they'll think their opinions and thoughts aren't valid. ALL children can do so much. Focus on what they *can* do, not what they can't. Research tells us that parents with high expectations tend to have children with better school outcomes.

Think about your childhood memories. What did you want or need at that age? How did it feel when people didn't seem to take you seriously or respect your needs? What do you still want or need? Is it that different from when you were a child?

> ▶ **Listen, love, and support.** Even if you're faced with challenges and situations you never expected to face with your children, they're always going to be your children. First and foremost, your children need your love and support. Listen to them, and ask them questions about their feelings, their likes and dislikes, their day. Brainstorm together to find solutions to the problems they're having, and encourage their interests. Keep listening and talking with them, keep loving and supporting them. The things we say and do now have lasting effects, even if children don't remember or can't put it into words later in life—children will remember the feelings of love, support, and security.

> ▶ **Give them choices.** Children are born with their own little personality and preferences. Encourage them to explore that, and offer as many choices as possible. Engage them with the ordinary household tasks. For example, as they get older, plan the week's meals together. Encourage children to make a drawing of the menu to remind them what they helped you decide to cook together. Worried they're always going to pick ice cream for dinner? Provide a few options for them to choose from, and listen to them as they explain what they prefer. They might have a point about being tired of eating the same thing, and they might think of a really great alternative.

> ▶ **Let them grow.** The wonderful thing about this age is that young children actually want to help you with chores and in other areas.

They want to contribute and show you all that they can do as a "big kid." You can encourage that by giving them responsibilities they can manage. Even babies can practice feeding themselves and putting toys away. Let them be as independent as possible and do as much as they can by themselves, helping them as needed and celebrating their accomplishments.

You're raising independent, resilient children who know that you support them. Your "baby" will always be your "baby," even as a grown-up.

Here are some book suggestions if you'd like to learn more:

Altmann, Tanya, David L. Hill, Steven. P. Shelov, and Robert Hannemann, eds. 2019. *Caring for Your Baby and Young Child: Birth to Age 5*. 7th ed. New York: Bantam Books.

Chapman, Gary, and Ross Campbell. 2016. *The 5 Love Languages of Children: The Secret to Loving Children Effectively*. Chicago: Northfield Publishing.

Christakis, Erika. 2017. *The Importance of Being Little: What Young Children Really Need from Grownups*. New York: Penguin.

Masterson, Marie, and Katharine Kersey. 2016. *Enjoying the Parenting Roller Coaster: Nurturing and Empowering Your Children through the Ups and Downs*. Lewisville, NC: Gryphon House.

Siegel, Daniel J., and Tina P. Bryson. 2012. *The Whole-Brain Child: 12 Revolutionary Strategies to Nurture Your Child's Developing Mind*. New York: Bantam Books.

Warmly,

*School-to-Home Connections*  Gryphon House

# Chapter 8:
## Setting Up Child-Friendly Spaces

Regardless of the curriculum or approach to teaching and learning that you use, the children should be at the core of every decision you make and all that you do. This includes how you create the most child-friendly space possible. You are like a little invisible elf setting all the magic up to encourage children's independence, play, exploration, and joy! Those are the most important ingredients for learning. The environment isn't just the tangible, physical things you see and the layout. The environment is also how the space feels.

When you walk into a room, you can usually get a feeling. What's the atmosphere like in your space? Is it warm and inviting? Is it overstimulating? Is it engaging and supportive? Are there spaces where children can explore by themselves or with one friend? Are there spaces where they can engage in activities with several children at once?

As you consider how to set up the indoor and outdoor learning environment, start from the children's eye level. What does the world look like from their vantage point? Can they see what's available for them to explore? Is the lighting too dim, so the space is dark and uninviting? Is it too bright, so that it lacks areas for focus on specific explorations or lacks areas with softer lighting for relaxation? Are children able to access materials independently, or must they ask for help? Are their creations and pictures displayed at their level or so high up that they have to crane their necks to see their work? Are there too many charts and pictures cluttering very brightly painted walls?

Take a step back and look at your space through the children's perspective. You can even crouch down to see what they really see from their eye level.

## Consider How Design and Furnishings Affect Behavior

Think about how the lighting, furnishings, and colors you use affect children's behavior. For example, intense fluorescent light can have negative effects on highly active children and make them more active (Jaffe n.d.). Fluorescent lighting can also cause headaches and eye strain because of the variation in the color and brightness in the bulbs. This results in a flicker that can't be seen but can affect the way eyes see texts, which can negatively impact some people's ability to perform visual tasks (Wilkins 2019). Natural light, on the other hand, has been shown to have much better effects. In a study of classrooms in California, children in classrooms with the most natural light had a 26 percent improved rate in reading and a 20 percent better learning rate in math when compared with children in classrooms with little or no daylight or natural light. Encouragingly, the study suggested that teachers could change the arrangement of furniture or other items to access more natural light in their rooms (Bennett 2019).

LED lighting can be used to create the same brightness as fluorescent lighting without flickering, and its cool-temperature light can help to improve the behavior of students who struggle with hyperactivity. It is more calming than other types of light, which helps students to focus. LED lighting also lasts for a long time and is also more eco-friendly (Bell 2020). Other lighting, such as incandescent lighting, specific lighting over activity areas, and skylights, can also be used to give the feeling of natural, calming light (Jaffe n.d.).

Color can affect mood, focus, and energy levels (Bennett 2019). While we tend to associate bright colors with childhood, using much softer shades and tints of colors found in nature, such as muted browns, blues, greens, creams, pinks, peaches, and roses, will create a more calming, welcoming environment (Bennett 2019; Jaffe n.d.). To avoid overstimulation and distraction, limit the number of items on the walls, as studies have shown that children in highly decorated classrooms are more distracted and spend less time on task than when the decorations were taken away (Fisher, Godwin, and Seltman 2014). As you think about decorations and limiting clutter and distractions in your learning environment, it might be helpful to consider the following:

- ▶ The purpose of the item
- ▶ Whether it supports or celebrates children's learning
- ▶ Whether it is relevant to what children are learning

- ▶ Whether it can be turned into something hands-on and interactive instead; for example, can a chart about shapes become shape cards that children can use for matching, sorting, and playing a memory game, and as treasure on scavenger hunts?

- ▶ Whether there is enough white space between items displayed so that children can distinguish between each item (Fisher, Godwin, and Seltman 2014)

Young children should also contribute to their space with their own ideas and meaningful contributions of their efforts and work. A good place to start when designing your classroom is to provide areas for children to engage in different kinds of play.

- ▶ Quiet, solitary play, such as in a library, writing center, art area or manipulative area, where they can read, write, act out different stories using puppets, paint, or complete a puzzle

- ▶ Play with a friend, such as painting or creating art with a peer at an art area or observing caterpillars become butterflies and then drawing about it with a friend

- ▶ Boisterous group play, such as building a huge tower with peers in the construction area; being passengers, flight attendants, and pilots in dramatic play; or exploring bubbles at the sensory area

## Use Learning Centers to Support Children's Development

Set up different learning centers or activity and exploration areas to support children's interests and development. Common centers might include the following:

- ▶ Construction: blocks, cardboard, and other building materials

- ▶ Sensory play: sand and water, shredded paper, shaving cream, dirt, and things that make different sounds or have different textures

- ▶ Library: high-quality children's books, both fiction and nonfiction, on a variety of topics

- ▶ Arts: visual arts materials as well as musical instruments

- ▶ Dramatic play: clothes and props in an area where children can pretend and act out the different things they're learning about

> ▸ Manipulatives: interlocking blocks, pattern blocks and tangrams, beads and strings, shapes, puzzles, and games

Other centers might include science, technology, engineering, and math (STEM)–related items and prompts. You could set up special invitations and prompts related to children's interests or a specific topic they're learning about. You can offer invitations and provocations to entice children to try something new within individual centers as well. For example, you can ask children to build a structure that would help the Three Billy Goats Gruff to cross the river safely; place mirrors and loose parts such as buttons, pebbles, twigs, and chenille stems to encourage them to make a self-portrait; or place puppets made from gluing laminated copies of their favorite characters onto craft sticks beside their favorite books so they can act out the stories and even come up with an alternate ending.

When you talk about centers throughout the week, highlight different things children have done in the centers, such as showing their artwork or discussing a project they are working on, to encourage other children to explore that center. Change the materials in the centers regularly so children can try out new things and remain engaged.

Add books and writing materials, such as clipboards with paper and writing utensils, to all areas to encourage children to research, write, plan, and draw. For example, put pads of paper and pencils in the dramatic-play area. Children can use them for taking restaurant orders, writing a note from a teacher to a parent, or filling out a prescription in a veterinary office. Put paper and markers in the construction area to encourage the children to draw building plans.

Not sure what to include in centers, even after observing the children's interests? Brainstorm with the children and get their ideas. Then let them help you to set the areas up and create props to go into the centers and areas over time.

Consider the flow and arrangement of the centers. Place quiet spaces, such as the library and the writing center or quiet manipulatives, close together. Place messier areas such as art or sensory near a sink for easy cleanup and handwashing. Put the construction area in a space where the children's creations won't be trampled or toppled. If you don't have space for centers, you can create mini centers and invitations for play in small boxes or containers that children can take and use at their seats or at a table. This is also a great option if there are health and safety concerns about sharing materials. During the COVID-19 pandemic, our students had individual materials such as playdough and did sensory play in small, individual containers.

Centers don't need expensive toys and gadgets to be engaging. They can be stocked with lots of household and reusable items and will be just as enticing and effective. Empty paper-towel rolls with slits at the bottom and top to make notches make great blocks. Large caps from detergent and other bottles can serve as blocks, manipulatives, or art materials. Stamps for paint can be made from sponges. Lots of sensory fun can be had with water, dishwashing liquid, and food coloring— just add a whisk and watch the bubbles grow! Outside, add some old containers, pots, and pans to make a mud kitchen and music wall. Plant flowers and herbs together so children can tend to them and watch them grow. Make simple bird feeders and enjoy observing the different types of birds.

## Encourage Independence

Consider how to help children be as independent as possible in their space. What are the common ways that you intervene to help, and are there ways to give them more independence and ownership over their environment? For example, give preschoolers access to child-safe scissors so they can open their snacks (while they also practice opening snacks with their fingers). Provide sturdy stools at sinks, toilets, and light switches to help them to reach without your help. Give them specific tips such as, "Turn the faucet off until there are no drips," "Sing 'Twinkle, Twinkle, Little Star' or another song while you wash your hands," and "Turn off the light when you finish," will help them understand how to take care of their environment and be more independent. Label bins and other containers with words and photos to show them where items belong. Create name cards and cards with the word and corresponding picture on binder rings to help them to start learning how to recognize and spell simple words.

Collaborate with the children to create an engaging and enticing environment where you can all explore, learn, and grow together.

Here are some suggestions for further reading:

Daly, Lisa, and Miriam Beloglovsky. 2014. *Loose Parts: Inspiring Play in Young Children*. St. Paul, MN: Redleaf Press.

Duncan, Sandra, Jody Martin, and Rebecca Kreth. 2016. *Rethinking the Classroom Landscape: Creating Environments That Connect Young Children, Families, and Communities*. Lewisville, NC: Gryphon House.

Isbell, Rebecca. 2008. *The Complete Learning Center Book*. Rev. ed. Silver Spring, MD: Gryphon House.

MacDonald, Sharon. 2001. *Block Play: The Complete Guide to Learning and Playing with Blocks*. Silver Spring, MD: Gryphon House.

Nicholson, Shelley, and Jessica Martinez. 2017. *Thrifty Teacher's Guide to Creative Learning Centers*. Lewisville, NC: Gryphon House.

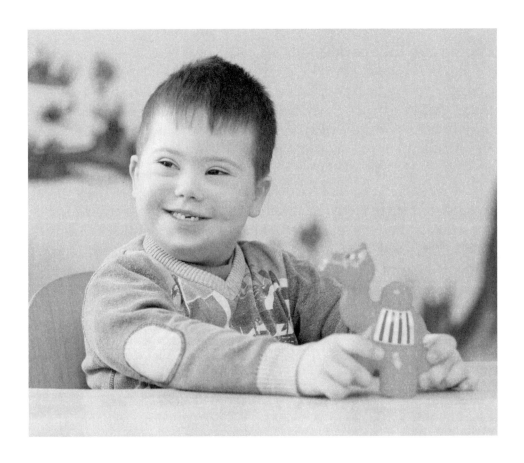

Dear Family,

It's easier than you think to create a child-friendly environment without losing control of your space and tripping over toys as you walk! Just as you need to feel at home where you live, children need to feel that their home is for them too—which can be difficult at times when everything is adult sized. It's especially important to give your children as much ownership over their space as possible as you empower them to become more independent and self-sufficient. They can do a lot more than you think, and sometimes, more than you want them to do. It's okay to let them begin to do things for themselves. They will still be your baby and will always need you for other things.

Collaborate to find a space in your home that they can make their own. They need a spot where they can play safely and can access their things independently. Creating little interest areas or "centers" will allow you to supervise without always having to play with them, especially if you need to get some work done. Consider some of the following ideas:

- ▶ Place books in one area as a mini library.

- ▶ Gather blocks or household items, such as empty paper-towel rolls, dried sponges, clothespins, old boxes, and containers, and make a construction area in a corner.

- ▶ Make a pretend-play area by gathering some fun kitchen tools and clothes for children to play dress-up.

- ▶ In a pot or sturdy container, add water, a few drops of dishwashing liquid, and a whisk so they can have a fun sensory experience.

With your children, decide on materials to add to extend play, and change the materials as their interests change.

Any child can help you to clean up after themselves if you set up a system to help them. Don't have shelves? Encourage them to decorate boxes, crates, and baskets for their toys and other items. You can create drawings, take photos, or cut out pictures from magazines together to label the containers so they know where to put things back.

Encourage your children to do as much as they can for themselves, and invite them to help out at home. When you start to see things through their eyes and brainstorm with them, it will surprise you how easy it will be to help children be more self-sufficient. For example, if they can't reach the sink to brush their teeth and tend to leave the water running, add a sturdy stool and remind them to turn the faucet until there are no drips. Is your child always fighting over what to wear? Organize their clothes in the closet or drawers by category: school clothes, dress-up clothes, or playclothes. Or perhaps organize by type of clothing: pants or leggings, skirts or shorts, shirts, and so on. Then allow your child to choose freely from the categories.

Remember to ask yourself, "Can this be done another way?" You might be so tied to your way you haven't even considered that their way works just fine—or even better!

Warmly,

*School-to-Home Connections*  GryphonHouse

# Chapter 9:
## Building Child-Friendly Schedules

Young children love routines and predictability, probably because it helps them to have some amount of control and understanding in a world where they may feel that they have very little control about what ultimately happens to them. Child-friendly schedules that consider children's needs and interests can help them and you to be successful.

## Set Up Flexible Routines

Setting up routines and a schedule doesn't mean you have to be rigid. Some space for flexibility and adjustments based on immediate needs and children's suggestions, such as children seeming to need more movement time before they can attend to a story that day, their focused and excited engagement in a new project, or the need to accommodate a special visitor to the class, should still be allowed. You might also capitalize on teachable moments and expand on an activity that really captures children's interests, such as reading a story about butterflies after children notice them during outdoor play and then mimicking butterfly movements to make a dance.

## Create Visual Schedules

Make visual schedules with pictures of the children engaging in the different activities to help them understand the routine and know what's coming up next. Sand timers and other timers that children can clearly interpret can help them prepare for and transition to other activities. Share your schedule with families so they can talk about it with their children and try to follow it during holidays or weekends. When possible, encourage families to follow consistent rest and mealtimes when at home. When my school was closed during the COVID-19 pandemic, one of the first things parents asked for was a copy of the schedule and help in understanding what their child did all day so they could engage them too. They even asked us to send the "magical nap time song" (a request I've also gotten on random weekend evenings from exhausted, desperate parents) in an attempt to get their child to nap at home.

## Respect Attention Spans

Remember that young children have very short attention spans. Each guided activity, such as during large- and small-group times, should be about fifteen to twenty minutes each for preschoolers and shorter for younger ones. Include at least an hour for purposeful play through centers or other child-led explorations plus an hour for outdoor play each day (Virtual Lab School n.d.). Balance activities where children are expected to sit, such as story time, with activities where children can move more, such as during centers or movement times.

The schedule should include not only teacher-directed time but also lots of time for independent play and exploration. During independent time, such as during centers time, teachers can observe, facilitate play and understanding, and act as play partners. Whole-group times can include morning gathering and sharing times, the introduction of new concepts or ideas that children will explore and learn more about, story times, and song times. Children can also gather in small groups for more in-depth exploration about something of interest through teacher-facilitated experiences or instruction.

Small-group time is also a great way to differentiate teaching and learning and support children's varying needs and learning styles. This doesn't necessarily mean that you will need to prepare a ton of materials for dozens of individual differentiated daily activities. You can usually use the same materials for differentiated instruction. For example, when doing a literacy activity, one group might just be introduced to the letters by using their fingers to touch sensory sandpaper letters or your homemade version using glitter glue or puff paint. Others who are ready to write might try writing the letters on their own, while others might start blending two letters to make simple words.

Schedules will also vary based on assigned times for certain components, such as a specific outdoor playtime or lunchtime, depending on the rest of the school's scheduling. For preschoolers, your daily schedule or flow for the day might look something like the following but should be tailored for your learning environment and to address your children's needs:

- ▶ Arrival and limited centers play

- ▶ Morning gathering and whole-group time

- ▶ Centers play (which might be combined with small-group instruction and rotations while the larger group plays in centers)

- ▶ Snack time

- ▶ Movement time

- ▶ Story time (which might include time for children to reflect and write or journal about the story or another topic, then to share with the class)

- ▶ Lunch

- ▶ Outdoor play

- ▶ Rest time (either nap or some quiet time resting before looking at books or doing quiet activities)

- ▶ Snack time

- ▶ Centers play

- ▶ Dismissal

Provide children with notice and cues, such as using a chime five minutes before and then one minute before transitioning to a new activity. Cues give the children time to prepare themselves to change activities. Creating other routines, cues, or rituals can also help children to feel comfortable throughout the day. Consider creating familiar greeting songs in which each child is named and welcomed. Use a dismissal song or schedule a little time to give children an opportunity to express gratitude for something during their day or time to pause and take a few deep, calming breaths together.

Schedules might change based on your observations of children's physical and emotional needs, so be flexible throughout your time together. For example, children might need a little outdoor playtime instead of centers play on arrival, so they can get some of their extra wiggles out. When I did after-care at the preschool I used to run, we realized that children had an easier time transitioning to going home when they were picked up during outdoor play or when they were engaged in a quiet center reading a book or drawing. They struggled with the transition if they were building or creating something with blocks, because they wanted to complete their creations. We couldn't predict when children would be picked up, so we couldn't give children enough notice to prepare them to complete their creations beforehand. Therefore, we modified the after-care schedule and available activities to avoid these triggers and support them in their transition home at unpredictable times.

Schedules and routines can be helpful roadmaps that allow children and teachers to be comfortable with their daily path. Yet, unexpected or planned pleasant detours, such as field trips, special celebrations, or spontaneous moments of unadulterated whimsy and joy might arise. Be open to these possibilities!

You can read more about early childhood schedules and the differences among types of activities in these resources:

Beaver, Nancy, Susan Wyatt, and Hilda Jackman. 2017. *Early Education Curriculum: A Child's Connection to the World.* 7th ed. Boston, MA: Cengage Learning.

Butler, Anne M., and Michaelene M. Ostrosky. 2018. "Reducing Challenging Behaviors during Transitions: Strategies for Early Childhood Educators to Share with Parents." *Young Children* 73(4): 12–18. https://www.naeyc.org/resources/pubs/yc/sep2018/reducing-challenging-behaviors-during-transitions

Epstein, Ann S. 2014. *The Intentional Teacher: Choosing the Best Strategies for Young Children's Learning.* Rev. ed. Washington, DC: NAEYC.

Koza, Wendy, and Jodene Smith. 2009. *Managing an Early Childhood Classroom.* Huntington Beach, CA: Shell Education.

Miller, Karen. 2005. *Simple Transitions for Infants and Toddlers.* Silver Spring, MD: Gryphon House.

Warner, Laverne, and Sharon Lynch. 2004. *Preschool Classroom Management: 150 Teacher-Tested Techniques.* Silver Spring, MD: Gryphon House.

Dear Family,

Families are so busy! With work, school, sports, and other activities; homework for older children; and household chores, it's amazing that we can find time to sleep or eat a meal! As a parent, you are the most important person in your young child's life. You are your child's first teacher, and you will always be an important guide and source of love.

Your little one thrives on routine and predictability, so try to establish a reliable schedule so they can anticipate and understand what will happen next. Give your child a heads-up before transitioning to another activity. For example, say, "In five minutes we'll have to clean up our toys so we can have dinner and then bathtime." If there will be changes to the typical schedule, such as a different person picking them up from school or a family event such as a sibling's performance before they go home, let them know ahead of time. This will help to prevent meltdowns and misunderstandings. If your child needs a little extra support, make a drawing of your schedule together, or take pictures so your child can refer to it when needed. (This is similar to the visual schedule the children use at our school.)

We've attached a copy of our schedule so that you can have an idea of what we'll be doing each day. You can see when key times, such as rest and meals, take place in case you'd like to get in sync with the school schedule during weekends and holidays. Feel free to connect with us with any questions you might have. Connect with other families as well, so you can exchange tips on staying calm amid the chaos!

Warmly,

*School-to-Home Connections*  Gryphon House

# Chapter 10:
## Encouraging Children's Individuality and Uniqueness

One of our teachers of the infants and young toddlers casually said, "You know, before this school, I used to just give children things to do. But now that we ask them what they want to do, I can see so much more of their personality coming out." When children, even the youngest ones, are given the opportunity to just be, you will see (and perhaps sometimes feel a bit like you are struggling with) just how much personality, choice, and uniqueness they have right from the start. Our infants and toddlers feel so comfortable in their environment that everyone who visits the center marvels that we can leave our room doors open and the littles never leave (except when they thought I was there to take them for a walk, as I often did during our after-care program).

I remember a teacher at a conference some years ago share her lab school's journey to adopting an approach more aligned with Reggio Emilia. She said the lightbulb went off for her when a child in her class pointed to all of the cookie-cutter turkey crafts they had made for Thanksgiving and asked her, "Which one is mine?" If children can't identify and own their creations, then what was the point in the activity?

Before our preschool opened, one of our teachers facilitated a foundation-funded project in inner-city Kingston, Jamaica, with the preschools in the community at their local STEM center. The children decided to do a project on hot-air balloons, and it was amazing to see their artistic representations made from recyclable and reusable household items or "trashables." Each creation they made from scraps of paper plates, paper, and cloth was unique, yet they were all very much hot-air balloons.

You can nurture children's individuality and uniqueness in your learning environment too. Let's take a look at some suggestions for how to do it.

## Let Children Lead

Give children, even the youngest ones, as much input as possible in the design and layout of the environment. Children can help to plan and set up centers, choose materials, decorate the space, and put up their artwork. You can achieve this in even the smallest spaces, such as some of the rooms we have in the Caribbean, by creating mini centers and activities in little boxes that children can decorate and have easy access to. For example, place loose parts such as bottle caps, pebbles, or buttons with playing cards for a mini math center. Children can place the counters directly on the images on the cards to practice one-to-one correspondence, use the counters to make a set with the corresponding quantity as the card they picked, sort cards by type, and practice adding and subtracting by picking two cards and using the counters.

Allow children choice and say in activity planning and implementation. For example, if you are using a theme-based approach, you can talk with the children about ideas for the next theme. Or you can get their input about activities and projects they'd like to do based on your observations of their interests and their preferences and suggestions. If children aren't forthcoming with specific suggestions, you can start the conversation by saying, "I notice that a lot of you have been pretending to be superheroes. And some of you have really been enjoying watching how things splash at the water table. For our next theme, do you think we should do superheroes or water?" Then, allow them to elaborate on these ideas as they get more excited. Continue to be open to their suggestions as the theme progresses. They might suggest adding string to the construction area so they can build Spider-Man's web, for example.

Provide children with roles and responsibilities within the environment that they can put their spin on. For example, children can decide how they'd like to set the table, lead morning greeting time, and select the story for story time.

## Respect Children's Individuality

Spark children's imagination and celebrate their individual flair by allowing them to express themselves as they'd like and to make their own creative choices. Provide a variety of materials and loose parts, and encourage children to use materials freely to create masterpieces. For example, if a child decides to paint a banana, remember that a banana doesn't have to be green (unripe like we cook it in Jamaica) or yellow. It can be any color the child chooses. When children tell you their favorite colors, know that it's okay if a child's favorite is "rainbow."

Recognize children's strengths and encourage them to share their talents with others. Every child has a special strength that can be shared and highlighted, which is especially important for children who might not be used to being recognized for something good at school or at home. Research tells us that if a child believes that their parent thinks they are bad or have made an unacceptable choice, then their sense of self and self-confidence could be negatively affected (Ascher Shai 2011). Every single child needs to shine every single day. You can help children to highlight special things they or their peers have done by writing them on sticky notes that go on a special board or in a special jar. Read these notes at the end of each day. Create group cheers or little signals that you and the children use to recognize others as they do something special throughout the day, such as a thumbs-up for sharing or snaps for persisting when things are hard. Allow children to share their achievements and something they're proud of with their peers.

What are some of the other things you can do in your specific environment to support children's individuality and uniqueness? How do you nurture your individuality in your environment and share your uniqueness with the children and their families?

Dear Family,

Isn't it amazing (and maybe daunting sometimes) to see how much personality and uniqueness children have, even from birth? Here are some simple ways that you can nurture and celebrate this without pulling your hair out!

- **Choice, choice, choice.** As a parent, it's important for you to support your children's independence and exploration so that their development isn't hindered. Research tells us that if a child believes that their parent thinks they are bad or have made an unacceptable choice, then their sense of self and self-confidence could be negatively affected.

  Choose your battles with your children wisely by giving them as much choice as possible, wherever possible. Even the littlest ones will want a say in things such as what clothes to wear and foods to eat. For example, you could let them pick their clothes for the day. They may choose some, ahem, *interesting* outfits, but they will feel confident and happy that they could do it for themselves. If you're dressing for a specific occasion, you can still provide choice by giving your child a few acceptable options. Incorporate choice into routines and schedules you make together. For example, if you are working from home or have to get a task done, you can provide them with options that they like to do while they wait: "You could build with blocks or draw a picture for Grandma, and I have to do some of my work. Which would you like to do first—build or draw—before we make lunch together?"

  Include your children in meal planning so that they are more likely to be invested in what they'll eat. Provide them with a few options to choose from at the beginning of the week. They can create a menu together with words and pictures so they know what you've decided on together.

- **Get creative.** Encourage children to express themselves in different ways. You can work together and allow them to take the lead as they make up silly songs, draw pictures together, or make up a funny play about your trip to the supermarket.

- **Recognize the awesomeness in their intentions.** Sometimes we can get quite distressed looking at children's actions through our grown-up eyes. The mess in the kitchen created by the banging-pot orchestra or the toothpaste they've smeared on your table could be ways they are trying to express themselves or help out. Asking your children about what they're doing will help you to see that they might have just been trying to play music to cheer you up or trying to clean the table with the only cleaning agent they know, toothpaste. Asking before assuming will help you and your child to find a solution that works for both of you while nurturing their uniqueness.

When you're not sure what to do, take a deep breath before you react and ask yourself, "Is this really an issue or is this just **my** issue? If it's just **my** issue, how do I let it go?"

Here are some great books to read with your children to help them celebrate themselves and others:

Acosta, Alicia, and Luis Amavisca. 2019. *I Love My Colorful Nails*. Boston, MA: NubeOcho Press.

Avis, Heather. 2021. *Different—A Great Thing to Be!* New York: WaterBrook.

Moradian, Afsaneh. 2018. *Jamie Is Jamie: A Book about Being Yourself and Playing Your Way*. Minneapolis, MN: Free Spirit.

O'Hair, Margaret, and Sofia Sanchez. 2021. *You Are Enough: A Book about Inclusion*. New York: Scholastic.

Pearlman, Robb. *Pink Is for Boys*. Philadelphia, PA: Running Press Kids.

Reynolds, Peter H. 2020. *Be You!* New York: Orchard Books.

Here's some suggested reading to help you to understand your children's uniqueness, including information on special needs:

Boone, Victoria. 2018. *Positive Parenting for Autism: Powerful Strategies to Help Your Child Overcome Challenges and Thrive*. Emeryville, CA: Althea Press.

Jacob, Jen, and Mardra Sikora. 2016. *The Parent's Guide to Down Syndrome: Advice, Information, Inspiration, and Support for Raising Your Child from Diagnosis through Adulthood*. Avon, MA: Adams Media.

Kranowitz, Carol. 2005. *The Out-of-Sync Child: Recognizing and Coping with Sensory Processing Disorder*. Rev. ed. New York: TarcherPerigee.

Taylor, John F. 2013. *The Survival Guide for Kids with ADHD*. Minneapolis, MN: Free Spirit.

Willis, Clarissa. 2009. *My Child Has Autism: What Parents Need to Know*. Beltsville, MD: Gryphon House.

With creativity and individuality,

# Chapter 11:
## Embracing and Celebrating Our Diverse and Beautiful World

Our twos-and-threes class included children with autism spectrum disorder (ASD) and cerebral palsy as well as typically developing children. The children worked together to carry out their tasks and help each other in ways that are unexpected for an age that is supposedly developmentally self-centered. One little boy in particular was the greatest advocate for all of his friends, bringing shoes for his friend with ASD and gently assisting him to do his tasks. He noticed without being asked and jumped into action whenever he could, seeing his friends as partners who might need help just like he does sometimes.

Young children don't know prejudice. They may notice and ask questions because they are curious but not because they are close-minded. They may, however, be influenced by the adults in their lives. They may pick up cues from the way their grown-ups interact with others. They may note the unspoken physical reactions to different situations and groups. Young children naturally learn from their grown-ups, which affects the way they see their world and the people around them. We must, therefore, examine our own (sometimes unrecognized) biases and feelings around diversity.

Take a look around your classroom and center. What does the environment say about your approach to diversity? Do the books you share represent and include different families, cultures, races, and abilities leading their everyday lives? Or do the few examples available seek to spotlight difference in a way that emphasizes "otherness"? Do you display images of people of different ethnicities and with different abilities just going on with their daily lives and working together naturally? Do you include dolls and toys that represent the people found in your environment and community?

In 2019, I visited the Romanian countryside for my friend's small wedding at his home. I noticed that his ten-year-old cousin, who was visiting from a very rural area, kept looking at me shyly. In broken

English, she tried communicating with me as we worked together to set up. Finally, on the wedding day she smiled at me and said, "You are beautiful." Later, I asked my friend if I was the first Black person she had met or perhaps seen (a slightly odd question in 2019 I know), and he responded that I probably was. I was, of course, flattered by her statement, but I was more touched by the sentiment and the meaning. If children don't have regular experiences to learn about—and with— diverse people in a natural way that focuses on our similarities and common humanity while celebrating the differences that make us unique, then we are losing important opportunities to help children to grow up to be respectful, tolerant adults.

In graduate school, a few of us started an after-school program for third-grade children at a nearby public school in Cambridge, Massachusetts. We invited other university students to share about their countries (including those who were from the area), cultures, and just about anything they'd like that was important to them and could be shared with children. They shared through games, food, and activities. It was so wonderful to see how excited the children were to play the different games and learn about different religions and cultures. The children themselves were quite diverse and represented different ethnicities, nationalities, and home languages. I remember smiling as a Muslim child whose family was from Pakistan got excited, hoping for chocolates as she played a dreidel game while the children learned about Hannukah. On the last day, the children were invited to share with their classmates their own cultures and things that were important to them. I still marvel at how seriously these eight-year-olds took this activity, proudly beaming as they shared food, clothing, and games. One child even led a teacher from Ireland in by the hand and said, "Tell them about Ireland." The children were just as proud of their friends' uniqueness as they were their own, happy to share and learn together.

Children develop empathy and an understanding and appreciation of difference through teachers and other adults who model how to care for others. Teachers can respond to children's natural curiosity by asking them authentic questions to help them to think about how they can respect and learn about others (Jones 2017). Teachers should also support each child's individuality so that they will develop confidence in themselves. We teachers have a responsibility to make all families and children feel safe and to help other families and children understand their expectations for respect and kindness (Ascher Shai 2011). The following are some ways that you can celebrate diversity in your environment.

## Let's Find Out

How can you incorporate diversity seamlessly and authentically into your everyday programming? Go beyond the typical culture study that involves a "child-friendly" and diluted skim of a cultural celebration. Instead, view different cultures through the lenses of different approaches to tasks, different opinions and debates, and pictures of people from different racial and ethnic backgrounds in your environment. For example, if the children are learning about construction, include photos of structures from around the world. If your class is doing a culinary theme or just baking for fun, look up recipes from a variety of cultures, or even compare how the same recipe varies by country or culture.

## Let's Collaborate

Provide children with opportunities to work together, support each other, and have their special talents and strengths highlighted. Children can help other classes too. For example, older children can brainstorm ways to support younger children in another classroom. In an effort to support the development of empathy in our mixed-age class of older three-year-olds to five-year-olds, we learned about how we could be community helpers in our school community. The children suggested ideas such as reading to the babies and creating art to decorate the twos-and-threes room.

Children can conduct group projects on different topics that they choose. They can research and create evidence of their learning. This type of project also helps children to work together and build important social skills. Even the youngest children can do simple investigations and be supported by teachers who provide key vocabulary words and highlight the wonders around them.

You can create class books on different topics, with each child getting a page to fill with their impressions, opinions, and ideas. A class book can show how each person can approach things differently, and it doesn't just have to be on generic topics such as celebrations or foods. Class books help children respect uniqueness and individual approaches to life, so involve the children in making suggestions for areas they'd like covered in the book, such as ways they travel to school, special silly talents they have, and their favorite stories.

## Let's Connect

Invite families and community members to talk about meaningful events and interests in their lives. This can involve both children and families and doesn't even have to be tied to a specific culture, religion, or event but could include hobbies, skills, and interests. Parents can introduce children and other families to special celebrations, cook something delicious together, make fun origami animals, or exercise and dance together.

Look for and take advantage of all of the opportunities to introduce children to our beautifully diverse world so that they can develop a deeper appreciation of others and themselves.

Want to find out more? Here's some suggested reading:

Alanís, Iliana, and Iheoma Iruka, eds. 2021. *Advancing Equity and Embracing Diversity in Early Childhood Education: Elevating Voices and Actions.* Washington, DC: NAEYC.

Christenson, Lea Ann. 2020. *Strength in Diversity: A Positive Approach to Teaching Dual-Language Learners in Early Childhood.* Lewisville, NC: Gryphon House.

Day, Monimalika, and Rebecca Parlakian. 2003. *How Culture Shapes Social-Emotional Development: Implications for Practice in Infant-Family Programs.* Washington, DC: Zero to Three.

Follari, Lissanna. 2014. *Valuing Diversity in Early Childhood Education.* Upper Saddle River, NJ: Pearson.

Iruka, Iheoma, Stephanie Curenton, Kerry-Ann Escayg, and Tonia Durden. 2020. *Don't Look Away: Embracing Anti-Bias Classrooms.* Lewisville, NC: Gryphon House.

Nicholson, Julie, et al. 2019. *Supporting Gender Diversity in Early Childhood Classrooms.* London, UK: Jessica Kinsley Publishers.

Dear Family,

You're never too young to learn about the wonders of our world and its people and to celebrate the diversity all around us. Learning about people and places beyond their own experiences helps children to grow up to be tolerant, respectful adults who also feel respected, empowered, and celebrated. It's also important for us to consider the sometimes unconscious biases in our words, actions, and everyday lives. For example, are the "bad guys" on the shows we watch usually of a certain race? Are we encouraging stereotypes in the way we describe others? Here are some easy suggestions to help your children celebrate the diverse and beautiful world around them.

- **Explore our community.** You can learn about the diversity that exists within our own community in many ways. Take walks to experience different places and events, such as street fairs and art or music festivals. Even babies and toddlers will enjoy walks as you point out interesting sights, sounds, and smells. You can also draw blueprints or maps of special community spaces, taste new foods, and look for signs or ways that people with different needs and disabilities are supported—and even come up with some solutions and suggestions of your own.

- **Let's celebrate!** Talk with your child about the different cultural celebrations or events your family enjoys doing together. Choose a celebration from another culture and learn about it together. You can even interview someone from that culture about it. You can also make up your very own celebration together and talk about why it's important to your family.

- **Help our community.** Talk with your child about different ways that you can be community helpers, such as offering to help to buy groceries for an elderly neighbor or donating old toys to a school or community center. *Simple Acts: The Busy Family's Guide to Giving Back* by Natalie Silverstein has even more suggestions.

Take advantage of all the wonderful opportunities both you and your child have to learn more about the world around you, and in turn, to learn more about yourselves.

We'd also love to learn more about our own little world. We'd love to have you visit and share something special about yourself with us. You can share a special talent, interest, celebration, food, or something you love about your culture or traditions. Please talk with us about what you'd like to do so we can schedule it.

Warmly,

*School-to-Home Connections*   Gryphon House

# Chapter 12:
## Supporting Social-Emotional Development

It's amazing how much even the youngest children can remember and how much they look forward to the special ways that you connect with them. A year after the COVID-19 pandemic initially closed our school and after-care program, one of our two-year-olds still asks me to go for a walk when I visit. She remembers that as the special thing we used to do during after-care when she was only a year old.

Children need healthy, dependable, and supportive relationships. They crave connection from the adults and peers in their lives, which can form a strong base for their social-emotional development and their ability to develop resilience. Knowing they have people who will help them to get up when they fall or face challenges helps them handle adversity. Being exposed to continuous adversity or stress can impede their development and have lifelong effects because of the physical, cognitive, and emotional responses to the stressors they face. A child who is supported as they encounter regular stress develops resilience and coping skills. However, a child who is constantly exposed to chronic, toxic stress such as those faced in abuse or neglect or living in stressful conditions are more likely to have health problems as adults, including depression, alcoholism, heart disease and diabetes (Center on the Developing Child).

Children not only learn through their own interactions but also from observing others. How do you interact with the children? How do they interact with each other? When children feel belittled, ridiculed, or blamed, this creates a negative environment. Strive to create a positive verbal environment where children feel that they are honored, respected, valued, and special (Meece and Soderman 2010).

Self-regulation skills—children's abilities to manage their emotions and behaviors—have some of the most significant effects—even more than intelligence—on children's later outcomes (Jung 2020). You can support building social skills by modeling, coaching, and guiding children to develop empathy as well as conflict-resolution and problem-solving skills. For example, ask questions such as "What do you think you could do to . . .?" Or coach children as they try to resolve a conflict by encouraging them to take turns explaining what happened and how they're feeling, and then asking them to think of a solution that would help both of them. These skills can especially be nurtured and supported in an environment where children are able to explore freely and play together (Jones 2017).

## Explore Emotions

Reading different books and stories is a great way for children to learn about themselves and others. Talk about characters' feelings and how they might be similar to or different from the children's feelings if they were faced with the same situation. Children might want to role-play their favorite stories in the dramatic-play center, so be sure to supply props and costumes to encourage this, or create simple puppets for use with the book in the library.

Children also get a lot of practice through play. As they pretend and role-play, they are working through feelings they might encounter in different situations and scenarios. Most of this play is based on their experiences and things they are learning about and trying to process, such as acting out or drawing about changes that are happening at home, such as a divorce or the birth of a new baby, or pretending to be the teacher reading a story to the class. Teach the children that it's okay to have all of their many different feelings, even the ones we might think of as "negative," such as anger and frustration. Also teach them that there are appropriate ways to handle these feelings so they don't affect the children and others in negative ways. Just like us, children can't reason with you rationally until they're calm, so give them a safe and soothing space to calm down before talking about what they are feeling and working together on how to move forward.

Help children to connect with their body's reactions to all of their different feelings so they are better able to recognize their emotions in different situations. Help them learn words to describe how they are feeling and to name their emotions, such as *happy, sad, angry, frustrated, grateful, proud,* and so on. They especially need to recognize what it feels like when they are calm and happy, so they can return to that feeling through different techniques and strategies. For example, when they feel stressed or frustrated, teach them to breathe deeply. Just taking three deep belly breaths can make a world of difference. Invite them to connect to their senses to help ground them when they're upset by pausing to notice what they see, what they smell, what they hear, and what they can touch. When littles practice calming strategies and techniques while they're already calm, they can more easily draw on these techniques when they need them. With practice, these practices will become second nature.

## Encourage Empathy

Children display empathy and prosocial behavior from a very young age. Researchers have shown that by the time they are one year old, children can show "empathic distress" by matching their emotions to others and crying when others cry. By the time they are eighteen months old, children will try to help someone they perceive as sad (Warneken and Tomasello 2006, as cited in Hyson and Taylor 2011).

Help children to become empathetic by introducing them to people who are different from them and who have different perspectives. Help them to understand that different people can respond to the same situation differently and it's everyone's job to respect others' feelings and find ways to support them. Most important, model this by empathizing with them first. For example, talk together about different situations, such as going on a roller coaster, and ask children to say how they might feel. Some might be scared while others might be excited. Even talking about favorite centers and games will help children to see that everyone has different preferences. Use stories to build on this by asking, "How would you feel if you were _____ and this happened to you?" Or model different interpretations of the same situation with a teaching team member: "I was afraid to go on the field trip because I'd never been on a big school bus before, but Aunty Winnie was excited because she loves buses and she told me it would be okay."

As grown-ups, we usually don't want people to immediately come up with solutions when we complain of having had a bad day. We just want them to listen, be on our side, and say, "That does sound like a hard day. I'm sorry today was hard for you." Do the same for your students and guide them as they learn to do the same for others. Even babies and toddlers want someone to recognize and empathize with their problems. One of our one-year-olds babbled angrily at a little girl who sat in the toy car she had been pushing. Her teacher vocalized her frustrations for her, saying, "I know! You're upset that she took the car you were using." She empathized with her and helped her to problem solve.

## Help Them to Problem Solve and Handle Conflicts Independently

Conflicts, challenges, and problems will always arise. Your role is to guide, mediate, support, and empower children to take ownership and eventually become independent problem solvers. Forcing children to say *sorry* to each other might only teach them that this word gets them out of trouble, not that they should use it to authentically express remorse. Instead, help them to work through their conflicts with their peers and others by allowing each child to share what happened. Then, ask them to suggest a solution. If they're new to suggesting solutions, provide suggestions they can use.

Problem solving is also important for individual challenges children might be having. Empower them to think of ways to solve their problems and find solutions they can act on. Helping children to become resilient requires teaching them how to recover from challenges and setbacks and reassuring them that they have a secure base, such as you and their families, to support, nurture, and encourage them. They can't become resilient if they are always shielded from difficulties that they could manage with your help.

## Support Each Child's Unique Needs

One of our five-year-olds was sometimes hesitant to come to school because he said that some of his classmates had hit or tried to hit him on the playground. However, the children had just been racing around loudly as they played a chasing game. The hesitant child is quite sensitive to movement and noise and had probably interpreted their flailing arms and noise as attempts to hit him. We talked with his concerned parents, who thought the children actually were hitting him, and adjusted our approach at home and school to help him to interpret the situations. We talked with him and helped him to step back and observe the children's actions so he could see that they were just being loud and moving their arms while they were running, even when he was not there. We also helped him to problem solve and strategize about what he could do, such as moving away or playing somewhere else, if someone did try to hit him or if they ran too close to him. By tailoring our approach to his specific needs, we helped to empower him to address the problem he was perceiving, rather than to see the others as the aggressors and him as the victim since that was not the case.

## Recognize Positive Behaviors and Encourage Gratitude

Specifically recognize and acknowledge positive acts, such as kindness, teamwork, empathy, and caring, so children receive positive reinforcement and others have guidance and specific examples of what they can do to be kind to others. For example, say, "Thank you for sharing your toys with your friend. He is smiling because he is happy you shared." This type of comment provides details about what children can do for others. Saying, "Be nice," doesn't provide any specific guidance at all. Also encourage children to express gratitude to each other for acts of kindness.

You are one of the children's greatest role models, and they'll learn so much from the tone you set and the way you handle your own emotions. Keep smiling and keep breathing as you coach them through your words and your actions. Here are some books and a website suggestion if you'd like to find out more:

The Center on the Social and Emotional Foundations for Early Learning offers free resources and tips for teachers and families: http://csefel.vanderbilt.edu/

Erwin, Elizabeth J. 2020. *The Power of Presence: A Guide to Mindfulness Practices in Early Childhood.* Lewisville, NC: Gryphon House.

Miller, Susan A. 2017. *Social Development of Three- and Four-Year-Olds*. Lewisville, NC: Gryphon House.

Welch, Ginger. 2019. *How Can I Help? A Teacher's Guide to Early Childhood Behavioral Health*. Lewisville, NC: Gryphon House.

Dear Family,

Children need healthy, dependable, and supportive relationships to nurture their cognitive and emotional development. Research tells us that being exposed to continuous adversity or stress can impede children's development and have lifelong effects, including depression, alcoholism, heart disease, and diabetes, because of the physical, cognitive, and emotional responses to the stressors they face. But children who are supported as they encounter regular stress develop resilience and coping skills (Center on the Developing Child n.d.).

Children's self-regulation skills—their abilities to manage their emotions and behaviors—have some of the most significant effects on their later outcomes, researchers tell us. Children learn how to develop healthy self-regulation when they have positive role models in their lives; that's you! Here are some ways that you can support your child's social-emotional development and self-regulation.

> **Practice calming strategies.** When they are very upset or having very strong emotions (which are perfectly normal), children can't speak with you or understand you rationally. They must first calm down. Help them to use calming strategies to manage strong emotions. For example, taking three deep breaths to make the belly inflate like a balloon on the inhale and deflate on the exhale can make a world of difference for children (and for you!). You can also help them calm down by connecting with their surroundings and senses. To do this, ask them to name things they see, smell, touch, and hear. Brainstorm other things that they like to do that can help them, such as drawing, dancing and shaking, singing, or just taking time away to breathe and hug a favorite toy in a cozy calming spot that you've set up together. The more children practice using these strategies while they are already calm, the easier it will be for them to use them when they need to.

> **Recognize how their body looks and feels.** Help children recognize how their body looks and feels when they're experiencing different emotions, such as happy, sad, angry, frustrated, proud, and so on. You can use a mirror so they can see what they look like. Then talk about the feelings in their body so they can connect with and notice them as they experience different emotions. For example, noticing that their stomach feels a little funny when they're nervous will help them to explain to you why they're resistant to doing something. Being able to recognize and name their feelings will help them feel calmer and in better control. You can read more about expressing motions in *Permission to Feel: Unlocking the Power of Emotions to Help Our Kids, Ourselves, and Our Society Thrive* by Marc Brackett. The Center on the Social and Emotional Foundations for Early Learning also has free resources and tips. You can find them at http://csefel.vanderbilt.edu/

▸ **Be a role model.** You are your children's first and most important teacher. They pick up on every expression, change of tone, and action you make. They learn more from your subtle, almost subconscious, behaviors than you think. For example, they notice whom you might like or dislike, how they should treat others, and how they should respond to different situations. It can be exhausting to think about, but it's true! So consider what kind of role model you want to be for your children.

▸ **Highlight kindness and positive acts.** Provide positive reinforcement that encourages children to be kind to others. Recognize and acknowledge ways that your children and others demonstrate kindness and compassion. For example, say, "Thank you for sharing your toy with your baby sister. She is very happy that you did," or "Our neighbor really appreciated it when we helped them to mow the lawn."

▸ **Anticipate and role-play difficult situations.** Help children handle difficult situations by talking about them and role-playing beforehand. For example, if children are nervous about a visit to the doctor, act out what will happen and remind them that you will be with them. If you are moving to a new home, help them get excited by planning their new space and talking about how they will stay in touch with people who might not live so close anymore. You can even practice having video calls before you move, so they can become more comfortable with the transition.

▸ **Read books.** Child-friendly stories and nonfiction books are great tools to help children learn about themselves and others. They can explore different emotions and responses through different characters and learn about other people, cultures, backgrounds, ways of life, and families.

Although it can seem daunting to keep your own emotions in check so you can be a positive role model for your children, just continue to be open, loving, and vulnerable. Admit missteps to them, and talk about how you could have handled something differently, such as calming down before speaking instead of shouting at someone. Children will learn that there's always room to grow and that you can both work together to support each other.

Sending you smiles,

*School-to-Home Connections*   Gryphon House

# Chapter 13:
## Language and Literacy

It can be particularly tempting to think that, while play is a nice filler for certain activities, more didactic, rote teaching practices are necessary for children to learn how to read and to develop their language skills. While some of these skills, such as letter knowledge, might require memorization, think about how you learn best. What piece of information did you recently learn and remember? Was it because someone forced you to recite it repeatedly, or was it a juicy tidbit or nugget of information that excited or piqued your interest enough that you remembered it?

Children can acquire the language and literacy skills they need through intentional interactions with you and their peers, and through authentic play and engaging experiences that nurture their desire to read, write, and converse with each other (Matijević and Bernić 2020). Think of ways that you can subtly infuse tips and information through your environment and interactions with children. When I was in college and volunteering with young children, I remember the moment something clicked in me about the importance of early childhood (something I wasn't even studying at the time). A little boy came up to me and showed me a picture of a firefighter in a book and asked if we could act it out and be firefighters too. Seize the moments and let your littles be your guide.

## Let's Read

Read a range of books together, and place related books in different centers to encourage children to reference them in their play. As you read books, poems, and other materials, point to the words so children start to develop the understanding that spoken words can be written and that words are made up of letters and separated by spaces. Pointing to letters also helps children connect the symbol (the letter) with the sound it represents. Reading books with predictable patterns or repeated phrases, rhyming books, and books with movements are also great ways to involve children in the reading process as they chime in and move along with you.

Books are also great springboards for children's interests and can spur them on to start projects. For example, they might be inspired to explore a different culture, how something is made, or the jobs that people in the community do.

## Let's Talk

There's a big difference between talking *with* children and talking *at* them. Is every conversation really just giving directions and instructions, saying no, and finding ways for you to lead? Or are you talking with your littles? Are they able to take the lead, to share their thoughts, opinions, and feelings freely? Are they asking and answering questions that require thought and more than one-word answers?

A study involving four- to six-year-old children found that, even though children from wealthier families tended to be exposed to more language than children from families with lower incomes, children from lower socioeconomic backgrounds who had families who spoke with them a lot had similar brain activity and language skills to those from families with higher incomes (Trafton 2018). Talk with the children, and encourage their families to talk with them too!

Set the foundation early for babies and toddlers by always using real words with them rather than made-up baby talk. Sing silly songs and describe everything around them so they start to learn the words even before they can say them. Developing your language skills also means learning how to converse with others by making eye contact and waiting for your turn to respond with a relevant remark. Talk and sing with children throughout the day. Even babies who can't talk can do this. As they coo and babble, you can then respond and match their tone and expressions with words.

## Let's Play

It's particularly tempting to dwell on letter recognition as a marker of children's developing literacy skills, particularly as that's probably the marker being used by their parents. But letters are not the "be all and end all" of language and literacy development. Before children can be successful readers, they need to also develop skills such as phonological awareness, so they can apply this when they come across a word they don't know but is similar to a word they've seen before. If they can rhyme and understand that words are made up of different sounds and can manipulate the sounds they hear then when they see a new word, children can draw on these skills to decipher new words. They can slowly read a new "big" word because they have an awareness of how words with many syllables sound.

All of this can be accomplished without even looking at a letter, through simple, engaging games, such as the following:

▸ Clap the number of syllables in children's names while you take attendance. (Hint: Every time your chin goes down, it's a new syllable: Bran-don).

▸ Make up silly rhymes and play silly word games together: After identifying the beginning sound of a word, create new words by changing it: *run, bun, fun, sun.* Work your way up to doing the same for the ending sound of simple consonant-vowel-consonant (CVC) words (*run, rug, rut, rub*) and then the middle sound (*rub, rib, rob*).

▸ As you teach letters and as children learn sight words, help them to remember the letters by air writing the word after looking at it.

▸ Play games by asking them to tell you the second letter in a word they saw. As they progress, you can ask them what would happen if they changed the first letter in the word to another: Change the first letter in the word *sip* to a *p*. What word do you get?

Successful readers also need to comprehend what they're reading so they can understand what they're reading and apply this knowledge to answering questions and making predictions. Help children develop these skills by making movies in their head of what you're talking about, describing, or reading. Help them to picture things by using descriptive words when defining new words, and make up stories together with lots of rich detail. For example, instead of saying that a watermelon is a type of fruit, you could include more details so it becomes a description rather than a definition: "A watermelon is large fruit with a hard, green covering and juicy red flesh inside with tiny black seeds."

## Let's Write

Incorporate print and writing throughout your environment and throughout the day. Write down children's responses on chart paper or the board as you ask the question of the day or during discussions throughout the day. Encourage children to write the first letter of their name or their whole name beside their thoughts.

Place enticing writing materials in all centers so children can plan out their building designs as they construct with blocks, make tickets for rides on a roller coaster in the dramatic-play center, or record their observations as they experiment with mixing colors while they paint. Their writing will be scribbles at first, but then you will see letters here and there. Eventually, they can move up to using inventive spelling to write the sounds they hear, such as writing "kt" for *cat*.

Support parents by inviting them to an event or workshop on language and literacy. Include samples of children's work so they can start to see and understand their progress and acquisition of skills over time.

Whenever you're in doubt as you support children's language and literacy development, go back to your base and how they learn best—through play and fun. When you plan authentic, intentional interactions and experiences with that in mind, you can't go wrong.

Want to find out more about helping children's language and literacy? Here are some suggested reading and websites:

Cox Campus (https://www.coxcampus.org/) and Reading Rockets (https://www.readingrockets.org/) offer free resources and courses.

Bardige, Betty S., and Marilyn M. Segal. 2005. *Building Literacy with Love: A Guide for Teachers and Caregivers of Children Birth through Age 5*. Washington, DC: Zero to Three.

Hammett, Carol T., and Nicki C. Geigert. 2007. *Read! Move! Learn! Active Stories for Active Learning*. Silver Spring, MD: Gryphon House.

Miller, Cathy P. 2013. *Before They Read: Teaching Language and Literacy Development through Conversations, Interactive Read-Alouds, and Listening Games.* Gainesville, FL: Maupin House.

Murray, Carol G. 2018. *Simple Signing with Young Children: A Guide for Infant, Toddler, and Preschool Teachers.* Rev. ed. Lewisville, NC: Gryphon House.

Nemeth, Karen N. 2012. *Many Languages, Building Connections: Supporting Infants and Toddlers Who Are Dual Language Learners.* Lewisville, NC: Gryphon House.

Raines, Shirley, Karen Miller, and Leah Curry-Rood. 2002. *Story S-t-r-e-t-c-h-e-r-s for Infants, Toddlers, and Twos: Experiences, Activities, and Games for Popular Children's Books.* Silver Spring, MD: Gryphon House.

Read, Amy B., and Saroj N. Ghoting. 2015. *Time for a Story: Sharing Books with Infants and Toddlers.* Lewisville, NC: Gryphon House.

Rosenkoetter, Sharon E., and Joanne Knapp-Philo, eds. 2006. *Learning to Read the World: Language and Literacy in the First Three Years.* Washington, DC: Zero to Three.

Vukelich, Carol, Billie Enz, Kathleen Roskos, and James Christie. 2019. *Helping Young Children Learn Language and Literacy: Birth through Kindergarten.* 5th ed. Hoboken, NJ: Pearson.

Dear Family,

Helping your child develop language and literacy skills is as easy as talking and reading *with* them, which positively affects their attitude toward reading. The number of back-and-forth conversational exchanges your children experience is even more important for their brain development and language skills than the number of words they hear—something they obviously can't get from just watching a screen or being drilled with flash cards. Keep the conversation going! All you have to do is talk *with* your children at all ages and promote back-and-forth conversation or turns based on their responses and yours. Even babies can engage in back-and-forth conversations. Respond to babies' coos and expressions with comments related to what you're doing and their expressions. For example, if you hear your baby coo and see a smile, respond by looking at your baby and smiling and saying something such as, "Yes, I'm making your favorite carrots." Wait for your baby to react and keep going with your conversation.

- **Talk together about anything and everything.** Ask open-ended questions, or questions that allow children to say more than one word to respond, which encourages their language development and critical-thinking skills. For example, instead of asking, "Did you like the book?" ask questions such as, "What was your favorite part of the book?" or "What do you think would have happened if . . . ?" Then keep having a back-and-forth conversation by building on children's responses.

- **Describe what you and they are doing so they hear new words and understand how to make sentences.** For example, say, "You are jumping really high," or "I'm stirring the broth in the pot for our soup." Don't be afraid of using big words. The more words children hear in context, the better! When you describe things with lots of details, it helps them to picture what you're saying and make a movie in their head that will be an invaluable comprehension tool. So add lots of descriptions as you're defining words or telling a story. Think about details such as size, shape, color, and movement. Play descriptive games together. One of you can describe a simple picture while the other tries to picture it in their head. For example, don't just say, "I see a brown dog." Say, "I see a large, dark, brown dog with long, shaggy hair that is panting loudly as he looks directly at me."

- **Play silly word games.** This will help children start to learn about the sounds in words, which will support them as they learn to read and come across new words. You can say words in different ways and have them guess what you're saying. For example, you can say *cat* by focusing on the beginning sound and the rest: /c/ –at. Or you can split all of the sounds: /c/ /a/ /t/, and ask them to guess the word, which is harder to do.

You can clap the beats (or syllables) in words as you say them. Start with one- and two-syllable words, such as *cat* and *zebra*. Work your way up to words with more syllables. Not sure how many syllables a word has? Touch your chin as you say the word (and encourage your children to do as well). It goes down every time you say a different syllable. Try it! *Ze-bra*: two syllables.

▸ **Identify sounds you hear.** In addition to learning letters and the sounds they make, children should also be able to identify just the sounds they *hear* in words. Start with the beginning sounds, such as /b/ in the word *big*. Ask questions such as, "What sound do you hear at the beginning of *cat*?" (/c/) "Can you think of other words that start with /c/?" Remember that *k* words would count too, because you're just focusing on the sound for now.

Then move to the ending sounds as they get older: /g/ in the word *pig* or /t/ in the word *cat*. Finally, ask them to identify the sound in the middle of a word, such as /i/ in the word *big*.

Have fun with sounds. Point out *alliteration*, words starting with the same sound, such as, "Guy gorilla got glue," in books and songs—or just make up your own.

▸ **Play rhyming games.** Rhyming games help children learn that rhyming words sound the same at the end, which is a skill that will help them read unfamiliar words as they connect them with words they already know.

- Work together to make up as many rhyming words as possible. You can say a word and find a rhyme (even a made-up word): *rig, fig, pig, big, gig, sig, mig, lig.*

- Play rhyming hopscotch. Draw a hopscotch game, but instead of numbers, fill each square with words. Hop to the rhyming words.

- Sing rhyming songs! It's okay to use made-up words too!

- Bored on the bus? Give clues for I Spy using sounds, rhymes, or syllables. For example, say, "I spy a fruit whose name starts with *A* and rhymes with *bapple*."

▸ **Write in the air.** When introducing new letters and, later, sight words, encourage children to write it in the air in front of their eyes or trace the letter with their finger. This helps their brain to remember how the letter looks. Try it with numbers too, or even when you're trying to remember something important, such as an important date or phone number.

▸ **Point to letters and words you see in books and all around.** Pointing to individual words as you read helps young children understand that a written word is a combination of letters separated by a space. You can play games by finding a specific letter on a page or while running errands. For example, look for a certain letter on labels at the supermarket.

▸ **Read, read, read.** Make reading with your children a part of your regular routine. As you're reading together, point to the words and talk together about what you notice in the illustrations and words. Look for clues to what is happening in the story. Ask open-ended questions, such as "Why do you think he did that?" Encourage children to make predictions based on what they've noticed in the book. For example, you could say, "Hmm, I notice that the clouds have been getting darker. What do you think will happen next?"

When in doubt, smile and think "tennis." Keep that engaging, back-and-forth conversation going for as long as you both can. We are always here to support you and talk with you about your children's progress and how we can work together to support them. Feel free to reach out to us with your questions so that we can plan events and other ways to connect with you.

Here's some additional reading if you'd like to learn more about helping your children's language and literacy development:

Laikko, Teresa, and Laure Laikko. 2016. *Talking with Your Toddler: 75 Fun Activities and Interactive Games that Teach Your Child to Talk.* New York: Ulysses Press.

Rebelo, Lane. 2018. *Baby Sign Language Made Easy: 101 Signs to Start Communicating with Your Child Now.* Emeryville, CA: Rockridge Press.

Warmly,

*School-to-Home Connections*   Gryphon House

# Chapter 14:
## Fine-Motor Development and Writing

Parents might be eager to see their young child writing because it's an easy, tangible indicator of learning. But if you help parents to understand all that goes into being ready to write, they will appreciate the steps and the timeline to do this. Sometimes I explain this to parents in terms of weight lifting. I ask, "If you want to lift 200 pounds, but you've never been a weight lifter before, where do you start? Do you just pick up the 200-pound weight and hoist it over your head?" Even the most muscular parent inevitably says, "No, of course not." We talk about having to first start with lighter weights and build up our strength over time so we can increase the weight and eventually get to 200 pounds.

When children are "just playing," they are doing the same thing. Toddlers and older infants like using interesting writing tools, such as crayons, colored pencils, and washable markers and paint to express themselves. These marks and scribbles will eventually turn into writing. Children are getting their hands and fingers ready to write as they roll out playdough, clip things with clothespins, and use tweezers and tongs. Even crawling helps to prepare children's hands for writing by helping to lengthen finger muscles, develop their hand arches, and encourage their fingers to be used for different purposes, just as they would in writing (BabySparks 2017).

Your interactions and encouragement during the early phases of writing play an important role in building children's confidence and views about their abilities (Emerson and Hall 2018). Don't bend to parent pressure and stress little hands before they're ready. Of course, children should have fun scribbling and drawing, but pushing them to copy and write identifiable letters and numbers before they're ready could turn them off of writing in the long term.

## Writing for Authentic Purposes

Place different types of writing materials and paper around the room and in different learning centers for children of all ages, so they can write for authentic purposes. Use the term *writing* when you're talking to them because their scribbles *are* their writing. For example, they can write menus in the dramatic-play restaurant, describe their artwork, sign their names on arrival (just like their parents do), interview their peers and interesting people for a project, journal about their day, and share thoughts about a special story, just to name a few.

Writing is a progression. They can use an unsharpened pencil to practice their pencil grip. As children begin to explore writing, they will progress from drawing and scribbling to including marks and lines that begin to resemble letters. Over time, they will randomly include letters and then begin copying words or writing letters to represent words. As children start to learn about letters and their sounds, they will use invented spelling to write a word. They may represent a word by the beginning letter, or they may write the beginning and ending letters, such as writing "mk" or "mlk" for *milk*. Eventually, they will progress to conventional writing (Byington and Kim 2017).

Encourage preschoolers and kindergartners to write lists with you. They can add a letter or mark to represent the sounds they hear in the words on a grocery list, such as *A* for *apples* or *MK* for *milk*. Point to the words you've written as you read the list, so they see that written words can be spoken and vice versa. When asking questions or taking polls, write children's responses on the board or paper, along with their name, so children see that their words have power and can be written down and read.

## Strengthening Little Fingers

Research tells us that children who engage in playful activities to strengthen their fine-motor skills have better fine-motor development (Suggate, Stoeger, and Pufke 2017). Between about twelve and fifteen months, a child's "writing" starts as scribbles, and then by about two-and-a-half to three years of age, they will start to draw lines and circles before they start drawing shapes that look like letters. Before first grade, children's handwriting is developing and might still look like scribbles as they learn to write letters and words (Zero to Three 2016). Instead of giving children workbooks and drills, allow them to enjoy writing, drawing, and making art so they can develop their love for writing.

Play, such as through the use of toys and manipulatives and arts and crafts exploration, supports children's fine-motor skill development. Here are some ways that you can help even the littlest ones to develop their fine-motor skills and a love for writing!

- **Playdough:** Encourage the children to use their fingers to play with homemade or store-bought playdough. Add cookie cutters and objects with interesting shapes, patterns, and textures for pressing, and use a thick, unbreakable bottle as a rolling pin.

- **Squeezy stress ball:** Add flour, baking soda, or rice to a balloon to make a simple squeezy stress ball. (Double up the balloons if children are particularly strong.) They can have fun decorating their squeeze toy too!

- **Self-help skills:** Help little fingers get stronger while they're learning self-help skills too! Encourage them to practice buttoning, zipping, and snapping their clothes. You can even make cheap dressing boards by gluing the edges of old clothes onto cardboard and adding shoelaces. Children can have fun practicing on the dressing board, or let them practice tying and lacing on a clean pair of shoes.

- **Tearing and cutting:** Even older infants and toddlers can prepare for cutting and using scissors by tearing scrap paper from magazines, newspapers, or circulars. When they're a little older, give children child-safe scissors, and supervise and encourage them to practice cutting paper. Use the little pieces as confetti for a party you plan together or to hide objects such as toys, letters, and numbers in the sensory table. Gradually build up to asking children to cut out a picture. Draw straight, curvy, and zigzag lines for them to try to follow as they cut.

- **Opening, closing, clipping, and more:** There are lots of household and low-cost items that can help children to develop their fine-motor skills.

  - They can practice opening and closing lids on nonbreakable containers.

  - They can press along the zippered line to seal bags.

- They can use tongs to pick up large and small objects.

- They can squeeze clothespins to pick up small objects or clip onto cards when playing matching games. Create simple matching games by coloring a clothespin to match a colored card, writing a lowercase letter on a clothespin to clip to the corresponding uppercase letter, or writing a number on a clothespin to clip to a card with that number of objects.

▶ **Action songs and fingerplays:** Singing action songs and engaging in fingerplays are great at any time of the day, including during unexpected downtime such as waiting for lunch to be served. You can play a game to think of as many creative ways to move your hands and fingers as possible—wiggle your fingers, close them, open them, pretend to be rain, make pretend fireworks, move them like a bird, roll them, move them in and out, tickle each other, and so on.

▶ **Sensory exploration:** Place some shaving cream, baking soda, salt, or dirt on a tray or in your sensory area, and let children use their fingers and have some fun exploring the material. Make a portable sensory bag by putting clear hair gel in a resealable bag. Add a couple drops of food coloring, and then seal the bag with strong tape. Place the bag on a table, and encourage children to use their finger or an unsharpened pencil to write on the bag. You can even put letters, shapes, numbers, and so on under the bag so they can practice tracing. If you want an easier, faster way to practice tracing, write something using a fat highlighter. Children can trace inside the highlighted word.

Invite parents to come play and try out different activities that strengthen little fingers. Ask them to think about their fingers and hands as they play. What do they notice as they roll playdough and clip with clothespins? Encourage parents and stand firm in the knowledge that the little ones in your care will be better equipped to be writers with the skills and strength they've gained through play.

Want to learn more about supporting fine-motor development and prewriting skills? Here's some suggested reading:

Isbell, Christy. 2010. *Mighty Fine Motor Fun: Fine Motor Activities for Young Children.* Lewisville, NC: Gryphon House.

Olien, Rebecca, and Laura Woodside. 2013. *Playful Writing: 150 Open-Ended Explorations in Emergent Literacy.* Lewisville, NC: Gryphon House.

Ray, Katie W., and Matt Glover. 2008. *Already Ready: Nurturing Writers in Preschool and Kindergarten.* Portsmouth, NH: Heinemann.

Dear Family,

When you are working toward a goal, you don't just hit your target immediately. You practice and slowly build up to your goal. For example, you track your number of daily steps and increase them over time. You gradually add more pounds to your weights until you reach your bench-pressing goals. You start off with simple recipes and learn the basics of food preparation before cooking something more elaborate.

The same thing happens for children as they learn to write. They first need to build up the strength in their fingers, hands, and wrists. Then they slowly learn the appropriate grip for holding writing tools. Research tells us that children who do more activities to strengthen their fine-motor skills have better fine-motor skills that will support later writing.

Between about twelve and fifteen months, children's "writing" starts as scribbles. By about the age of two-and-a-half to three years, they will start to draw lines and circles before they start drawing shapes that look like letters. Before first grade, children's handwriting is developing and might look like scribbles as they learn to write letters and words. Instead of workbooks and drills, just allow them to enjoy writing, drawing, and making art with you so they can develop their love for writing. Play supports children's fine-motor skill development, so encourage your children to play with and explore items you have at home. You don't need costly equipment or materials. Just allow your children to explore and play in their environment and with the materials they have.

- ▶ **Rolling, rolling, rolling:** Invite your children to help you to roll out pastry made with flour and water or to play with homemade or store-bought playdough. They can use thick, unbreakable bottles as rolling pins and press objects with different textures and shapes into the playdough.

- ▶ **Squeezy, squeezy:** Add flour, baking soda, or rice to a balloon to make a simple squeezy stress ball. (Double the balloon if your child is particularly strong.) Children can have fun decorating their squeeze toy with a permanent marker.

- ▶ **All buttoned up:** Help little fingers get stronger while your child learns self-help skills too! Encourage them to practice buttoning, zipping, and snapping their clothes. You can even make a dressing board by gluing the edges of old clothes onto cardboard so they can have fun practicing. Add laces or let them practice on your shoes.

*School-to-Home Connections*   Gryphon House

- **Tear it up, then cut it out:** Even older infants and toddlers can prepare for cutting and using scissors by tearing scrap from old magazines, newspapers, or circulars. When they're a little older, give your children child-safe scissors, and supervise and encourage them to practice cutting paper. Use the little pieces as confetti for a party you plan together. As their skills grow, build up to asking them to cut out a picture. Then draw straight, curvy, and zigzag lines for them to try to follow as they cut.

- **Everyday objects:** Your home is full of objects that can help little fingers get strong. Your child can practice opening and closing lids on nonbreakable containers, press along the zippered line to seal bags, help you to hang clothes out by squeezing clothespins, and use tongs (or clothespins) to pick up small objects such as cotton balls.

- **Fingerplay:** Sing songs and engage in fingerplays. These activities aren't just for silly fun but help to strengthen your child's hands and fingers and can be done anywhere! So the next time your child is bored on the bus, sing "Open, Shut Them" or "Itsy Bitsy Spider." Let your itsy bitsy spider go crazy climbing up the water spout, or just have fun moving your hands and fingers in as many creative ways as you can think of—wiggle your fingers, close them, open them, pretend to be rain, fireworks, a bird, roll them, move them in and out, or tickle each other.

- **Sensory play:** Children get excited about making marks and scribbles in fun sensory materials. Place some shaving cream, baking soda, salt, or dirt on a tray or large plate, and let them have fun using their fingers or an unsharpened pencil to explore. Make a portable sensory bag by putting clear hair gel in a resealable bag and then adding a couple drops of food coloring. Seal the bag with strong tape. Place the bag on a table so that your child can use their finger or an unsharpened pencil to write on the bag. You can even put letters, shapes, or numbers under the bag so they can practice tracing.

- **Writing:** Give your little one, even toddlers and older infants, interesting writing tools, such as crayons, colored pencils, washable markers, and paint, so they can enjoy expressing themselves with their marks. These scribbles will eventually turn into writing. Encourage your preschooler and kindergartner to write lists with you. Don't expect correctly spelled full words—not yet! Instead, they can add a letter or mark to represent the sounds they hear in the words on the grocery list, such as *A* for apples or *MK* for milk. Point to the words you've written as you read the list, so your child can see that written words can be spoken and vice

*School-to-Home Connections*   Gryphon House

versa. If you want an easy way to help your child to practice tracing, write something using a fat highlighter and they can trace inside the highlighted word.

Don't worry, just let those little fingers explore, move, roll, cut, wiggle, squeeze, scribble, hold, and have fun and they'll be strong (and happy) writers when they're ready!

Warmly,

*School-to-Home Connections*    Gryphon House

# Chapter 15:
## Physical Development

We can sometimes assume that our main responsibility as teachers is to consciously support children's cognitive and social-emotional development and that their physical development will fall into place naturally because they're already such energetic movers. However, it's still important to consider your role in helping children to develop physically, particularly as nearly one in four children between the ages of two and five years in the United States are overweight or have obesity (United States Department of Health and Human Services 2017).

Play is integral to children's physical development and well-being as it contributes to the growth of their motor skills and ability to engage in physical activities that will help them lead healthier lives (Venetsanou and Kambas 2010, as cited in Dinkel and Snyder 2020). Moreover, physical activity allows children to be playful and creative, problem solve, and cooperate and work in teams, as well as calm down and relieve stress (Gehris et al. 2018).

### Let's Get Moving

Preschool-aged children should be active throughout the day (Centers for Disease Control and Prevention 2021). Encourage movement throughout the day, not only for children's physical health but also for their mental health (and yours). Incorporate movement into transitions, such as moving in silly ways to go to the bathroom, having a dance break in between activities, or encouraging children to copy you as you make quick movements and then slow and calm movements as you settle down to listen at story time.

### Go Outdoors

Embrace outdoor play and provide children with as much time as possible to be outdoors playing and moving freely. Even infants and toddlers should have time outdoors, which also helps them to develop a healthy immune system (Norton 2020).

Play equipment to enhance outdoor play doesn't have to cost a fortune. Include large balls, ask handy parents or community members to make a balance beam or music wall with pots and pans, add a few large plastic hoops, and make obstacle courses with different objects. Children can explore loose parts from nature, such as a mud kitchen with old pots, sand, water, shells, pebbles, and kitchen utensils, and they can hop over cut sections of tree trunks or flat stones.

## Cross the Midline

During the day, include simple activities that encourage children to cross their midline—reach across their body from left to right or vice versa. This helps the left and right sides, or hemispheres, of the brain to communicate with each other and work together to help children as they move and learn (Blackmore 2021). Crossing the midline is an important skill for coordinating and executing everyday tasks, such as establishing a dominant hand and carrying out fine-motor skills such as tying shoes, playing games, and for tracking print from left to right. When children experience challenges crossing the midline, they might develop poor writing skills as they have not strengthened and refined the movement of one dominant hand. They might also have trouble reading text from left to right (Kid Sense 2021; Richmond and Marks 2019).

Invite the children to do windmills and touch their toes with the opposite hand, twist and wiggle their arms from side to side, kick or throw a ball that is placed off center, bang instruments such as a tambourine or blocks together in the midline, or reach for objects on the opposite side.

## Express Yourself

Celebrate children's creative expression through movement, song, play, and role-play. The more children connect with—and use—their bodies for creative expression and other activities, the more in sync they will be with the link between their body and their emotions.

Asking children, "How does your body feel?" can be such a powerful question as they start to learn about the connections between their bodies and their emotions and behavior. Helping children identify how their unique body reacts to certain situations and feelings will help them to identify triggers and warning signs and self-regulate.

## Eat Up

The early years are a wonderful time to set the foundation for healthy eating habits. Resist the urge to pressure little ones to take one more bite or sip, because this can inhibit their ability to self-regulate and listen to their bodies for cues about being full (Orrell-Valente et al. 2007).

In our school, children used to work together to make something special for birthday celebrations, and they enjoyed their sugar-free fruit popsicles because they made them. You can grow a small garden (herbs can even be grown indoors) and then make a simple meal together. In the dramatic-play center, children can role-play being at restaurants, farmer's markets, farms, gardens, or other food-related locations. They can build these locations with blocks or other items, write menus, and design their own diagrams of what they should eat each day.

## Read Together

Books are a wonderful way to help children learn about their bodies, different types of sports, exercises, and food. Reading both nonfiction and fiction books can spark children's interests in how they develop and be a catalyst for trying out healthy recipes and foods at school.

Get parents moving at a parent night or workshop with a mini yoga, aerobics, or other class. Then, serve or demonstrate how to make healthy foods (or have a healthy-food potluck), and encourage parents to ask their questions to a pediatrician, dietitian, or other expert who can provide information and simple tips for them as well.

Simple food swaps and incorporating movement throughout the day will make a huge difference not only to the children's physical and mental health but to yours as well.

Here's some suggested reading to find out more:

Connell, Gill, and Cheryl McCarthy. 2013. *A Moving Child Is a Learning Child: How the Body Teaches the Brain to Think (Birth to Age 7).* Minneapolis, MN: Free Spirit.

Michals, Deborah K. 2013. *Math and Literacy: Active Learning for Preschoolers.* Up, Down, Move Around series. Lewisville, NC: Gryphon House.

Michals, Deborah K. 2013. *Nutrition and Motor Skills: Active Learning for Preschoolers.* Up, Down, Move Around series. Lewisville, NC: Gryphon House.

Newman, Joye, and Miriam P. Feinberg. 2015. *Move to Learn: Integrating Movement into the Early Childhood Curriculum.* Lewisville, NC: Gryphon House.

Pica, Rae. 2001. *Wiggle, Giggle & Shake: 200 Ways to Move and Learn.* Silver Spring, MD: Gryphon House.

Sanders, Steve. 2015. *Encouraging Physical Activity in Preschoolers.* Moving Matters series. Lewisville, NC: Gryphon House.

Stamm, Jill. 2016. *Boosting Brain Power: 52 Ways to Use What Science Tells Us.* Lewisville, NC: Gryphon House.

Tortora, Suzi, and Claire Lerner. 2004. *On the Move: The Power of Movement in Your Child's First Three Years.* Washington, DC: Zero to Three. https://www.zerotothree.org/resources/316-on-the-move-the-power-of-movement-in-your-child-s-first-three-years

Dear Family,

You can support your child's physical development by encouraging them to move—as if they needed your encouragement! According to the Centers for Disease Control and Prevention, preschool-aged children should be active throughout the day. Physical activity allows children to be playful and creative, problem solve, cooperate and work in teams, and calm down and relieve stress.

▶ **Play, play, and play some more!** As young children play, they'll naturally move around, particularly as they role-play and engage in games such as tag or catch, go through obstacle courses, or play different types of sports.

▶ **Dance, dance, dance!** Have fun dancing together and coming up with silly moves. You can even make up moves to describe new words they're learning. This is also a great way for children to practice crossing their midline (reaching across their body from left to right or vice versa), which is a skill they'll need for reading from left to right and tying their shoes, among other activities. Have fun twisting and using your hand to touch your toes or other body parts on the opposite side of your body. Listen to different types of music and try dancing in different styles. Not only will you have fun, but you'll have a wonderful opportunity to introduce your children to different cultures.

▶ **How does your body feel?** Sometimes we are so busy going, going, going that we don't stop to really think about how our body feels, which can tell us a lot about how we're doing. Encourage your children to pause sometimes and think about how their body is feeling. What do they notice? Ask about different body parts or senses to help them to focus. For example, ask, "How does your tummy feel?" or "How does your heart feel?" This helps them to describe what's happening when they're not feeling well. If your child isn't talking, you can say, "Point to the part that hurts," or "Smile if your body is feeling good."

▶ **Try new foods.** Young children can be very picky eaters, but have no fear! When they're hungry, they'll eat. Try different foods, plan meals with them, and cook together so they have some say in what they're eating. Take note of what they like and don't like. Try not to mix new foods together because it will be hard to tell if they've rejected the entire meal or if there's only one thing they don't like that's mixed up with all of the other foods. When you're playing together, pretend to eat different types

*School-to-Home Connections*   Gryphon House

of foods, go to restaurants, or grow foods, so they can role-play how fun it is to eat delicious things.

If you're really concerned that your child is not getting enough nutrients, talk with the doctor to get suggestions and the teacher about eating habits at preschool. Sometimes picky eaters at home are happily eating everything at school because their friends are. Resist the urge to make children take one more bite or sip, particularly if they might have eaten enough and could be full. Children need to listen to their bodies telling them they're full or a drink is too sweet; this is how they learn to self-regulate.

▸ **Create a rest routine.** Even if your child isn't a napper, it's important that their body gets rest during the day. That can mean setting a rest or quiet-time routine where your child does quiet activities such as looking at books, drawing while listening to relaxing music, practicing breathing exercises, or trying some calming yoga poses. Set a bedtime routine that helps your child wind down, for example, a calming bath and story time with you before sleep time. If your child is resistant to bedtime, talk with your child and make notes to see what kinds of trends you might notice. Some children are afraid of the dark and just need a nightlight, or certain events such as rowdy play too close to bedtime may prevent young children from going to sleep.

▸ **Be a role model.** Children look to their parents for guidance on what they should be doing. Go for walks, have dance parties, grow and cook healthy foods together, get regular medical checkups, and get rest (which can even include pausing together for a couple of minutes to close your eyes, take deep breaths, and reset together).

Helping your children to honor their bodies' needs is critical to their physical and emotional development and will remind you just how important it is for you to do the same!

Warmly,

# Chapter 16:
## STEM for Young Children

STEM, which stands for science, technology, engineering, and mathematics, is a buzz term that can sometimes seem intimidating and make you question whether you need to get a PhD in physics to teach it. You may even have heard of STEAM and STREAM, which are STEM with the addition of the arts (A) and writing or reading or sometimes relationships (R). But don't worry! You don't need graduate school to provide intriguing STEM activities for children. All you need is curiosity, the ability to listen to children's questions, and the willingness to explore with them.

Research tells us that children who have foundational STEM activities and experiences at an early age develop the tools and confidence necessary to approach STEM activities and instruction later on in a more confident and curious manner (Early Childhood STEM Working Group 2017). You can integrate these activities in your classroom through hands-on projects based on children's interests and needs, giving children opportunities to use their inquiry and problem-solving skills and focus on their process rather than content knowledge. For example, children can use these skills to solve common problems or challenges in the classroom (Linder and Eckhoff 2020). They might devise a way to take turns using their favorite equipment on the playground. If they keep bumping into each other when playing in centers, they might help the teacher to design a better classroom layout. They might decide on the herbs they'd like to grow in a garden and then plant them and observe them as they grow before using them to prepare a snack together. Simply put, when children have authentic, hands-on play experiences that allow them to explore and manipulate and to have thoughtful conversations with you, then STEM/STEAM/STREAM learning will come out.

I like this description of STEM adapted from the Boston Children's Museum (2013, as cited in Parkes 2015):

- ▶ **Science is a way of thinking.** Science is observing and experimenting, making predictions, sharing discoveries, asking questions, and finding out how things work.

- **Technology is a way of doing.** Technology is using tools, being inventive, identifying problems, and making things work.

- **Engineering is a way of doing.** Engineering is solving problems, using a variety of materials, designing and creating, and building things that work.

- **Math is a way of measuring.** Math is sequencing, patterning, and exploring shapes, volume, and size.

To add arts to STEM, children can create visual representations of their work, role-play, dance, sing—you name it—to express their learning. By the time we add in the *R* of reading, (w)riting, or relationships, we seem to have all of the components of a well-rounded play-based approach to teaching and learning. Don't let the terms scare you—you've got this!

## Critical Thinking and Problem Solving

To integrate STEM in your everyday practices, start by asking open-ended questions. These are questions that require children to say more than one or two words and do not have a right or wrong answer. Asking these types of questions encourages children to think and share their opinions while developing their language and reasoning skills.

Ask questions starting with *what, how,* and *why:*

- What do you think will happen next?

- Why do think the raisins start to dance when you added the vinegar to the baking soda?

- How do you think we might be able to get the car to get from here to there in a shorter time?

- How can we test that?

- How do you know?

Children can make and record predictions about what they think will happen and then compare these predictions to the results. Provide children with opportunities for them to problem solve. For example, they can brainstorm ways to share the paint, manage a center that is overcrowded, or think of solutions for characters with dilemmas in storybooks.

Incorporate mathematical thinking and language into your daily routines by being intentional about the words you use and the opportunities you provide. For example:

- ▸ Ask children to set the table for lunch so they can learn about one-to-one correspondence.

- ▸ Have fun counting how many times they jump on the trampoline.

- ▸ Ask children to estimate the number of footsteps between their chair and the bathroom, and then measure it and compare each person's response.

- ▸ Sing different songs that incorporate mathematical thinking, such as "Johnny Works with One Hammer," "Sally the Camel," "Five Green and Speckled Frogs," and "The Ants Go Marching."

- ▸ Measure ingredients while you cook together.

- ▸ Compare using words such as *longer, shorter, bigger, smaller, heavier*, and *lighter*.

## Manipulating Materials

Provide materials for children to manipulate and explore as they design, build, and create. Simple loose parts such as paper-towel rolls cut into different lengths (you can even add slits around the edge if you want to get fancy and help them to connect), tree cookies, small pipe fittings, cardboard boxes, and other items from the hardware store can provide children with ample, budget-friendly options for endless exploration.

For young children, technology doesn't just mean electronic devices; it can also mean simple tools that they use during hands-on experiences. They can compare the effectiveness of different tools in carrying out a task. For example, is a ruler or a measuring tape more effective in measuring the length of a piece of paper? Which works best to measure the distance from the front door to the bathroom?

Just like the stem of a plant helps it to grow, STEM skills will help children develop in all areas, and all it takes is for you to encourage curiosity, exploration, and intentional play!

Interested in learning more about STEM? Here's some suggested reading:

Ardizzone, Leonisa. 2014. *Science—Not Just for Scientists! Easy Explorations for Young Children.* Lewisville, NC: Gryphon House.

Anderson, Sally, with the Vermont Center for the Book. 2012. *Math and Science Investigations: Using Children's Books to Make Big Discoveries.* Lewisville, NC: Gryphon House.

Connors, Abigail Flesch. 2017. *Exploring the Science of Sounds: 100 Musical Activities for Young Children.* Lewisville, NC: Gryphon House.

Cunningham, Debbie, Joy Lubawy, and Robert A. Williams. 2005. *Preschool Math.* Lewisville, NC: Gryphon House.

Davis, Beth R. 2015. *Hands-On Science and Math: Fun, Fascinating Activities for Young Children.* Lewisville, NC: Gryphon House.

Eckhoff, Angela. 2018. *Creative Investigations in Early Engineering and Technology.* Lewisville, NC: Gryphon House.

Eckhoff, Angela. 2018. *Creative Investigations in Early Science.* Lewisville, NC: Gryphon House.

Eckhoff, Angela. 2020. *Provoking Curiosity: Student-Led STEAM Learning for Pre-K to Third Grade.* Lewisville, NC: Gryphon House.

Englehart, Deirdre S., Debby Mitchell, Junie Albers-Biddle, Kelly Jennings-Towle, and Marnie Forestieri. 2016. *STEM Play: Integrating Inquiry into Learning Centers.* Lewisville, NC: Gryphon House.

McLennan, Deanna P. 2020. *Joyful Math: Invitations to Play and Explore in the Early Childhood Classroom.* Portsmouth, NH: Stenhouse.

Williams, Robert, Elizabeth Sherwood, Robert Rockwell, and David Winnett. 2010. *The Preschool Scientist: Using Learning Centers to Discover and Explore Science.* Lewisville, NC: Gryphon House.

Dear Family,

You might have heard terms such as STEM or STEAM and wondered what they mean. STEM simply means science, technology, engineering, and mathematics, with the addition of the arts (A) in STEAM. You may wonder whether you'll need a degree in physics to help prepare your child for the work world. Have no fear! Through play (yes, play!), children can get all of the foundational skills they need to explore these topics. And you can help!

Play with your children as they design, build, and create. Let them sketch out or draw a plan for their creation. Then, provide simple household items, such as empty paper-towel rolls cut into different lengths (you can even paint them and add slits around the edges to help them slot in), empty yogurt cups, cardboard boxes, small pipe fittings, and other items from the hardware store, for endless exploration.

While you are playing with your child, ask open-ended questions—questions that do not have a right or wrong answer and cannot be answered with just one or two words. Open-ended questions encourage young children to think and share their opinions while developing their language and reasoning skills. Ask questions starting with *what, how*, and *why,* such as:

- ▶ What do you think will happen next?

- ▶ Why did the raisins start to dance when you added the vinegar to the baking soda?

- ▶ How do you think we might be able to get the car to get from here to there in a shorter time?

- ▶ How can we test that?

Encourage your child to have a say and become a problem solver in your home. For example, they can think of ways to share a toy with a sibling, plan their pre-bedtime routine, brainstorm alternatives for dinner if an ingredient is missing, or think of solutions for characters with dilemmas in storybooks.

STEM is a great way to unleash your inner child as you let your little one's questions and curiosity lead you! To find out more, you can read *Math Right from the Start: What Parents Can Do in the First Five Years* by Jan Greenberg and Toni S. Bickart or *Where Does My Shadow Sleep? A Parent's Guide to Exploring Science with Children's Books* by Sally Anderson with the Vermont Center for the Book.

Inquisitively,

*School-to-Home Connections* **Gryphon** House

# Chapter 17:
## Nurturing in Nature

There is an expression in Norway, where I went to high school, that roughly translates to "There's no such thing as bad weather, only bad clothing." While some in other countries are fearful of rain and snow, in Jamaica where I live, many fear dirt and grime from hot, sweaty days outside. During our school's preopening professional development, one of our preschool teachers shuddered at the idea of taking the babies outside to sit on blankets on the grass during outdoor play. These days, the children in her class play outside and then pick up their shoes and race, crawl, get pushed in strollers, toddle, or get carried inside filled with dirt and the biggest smiles you've ever seen. It's a wonder their parents haven't sent us their laundry bills. Most of our new walkers take some of their first few steps on our patio or the playground beside it.

A study in Finnish day cares found that young children who were exposed to more natural environments and nature had improved immune systems (Norton 2020; Roslund et al. 2020). Children need time in nature. Not having enough time outdoors can negatively affect children's physical, emotional, and mental health and development. Conversely, children's physical, emotional, and mental health and development are supported by experiences in nature. Outdoor play and exploration also helps children develop a love and respect for nature that will later affect the way they see their role in preserving nature (Omidvar et al. 2019). So get outside and play! If a parent questions you, you can quote Aki Sinkkonen, one of the Finnish researchers: "I highly recommend letting children play in the dirt" (Norton 2020).

Bringing the outside in is another way to include free, open-ended manipulatives and materials. This can be as easy as creating sensory bottles with different items, such as leaves, stones, grass, and twigs, so children can explore how they look and sound when shaken and twirled. Here are some other easy ways to incorporate nature:

> ▶ Let children play freely! Embrace the mess, embrace the dirt! Set up a mud kitchen with pots, pans, old muffin tins, and other items for children to explore and use to make a "yummy" mess.

▶ Observe nature on your playground, during nature walks, or even in the classroom. Children can record what they notice in individual notebooks or on paper, and you can create class books with children's contributions. Learn about our spider and insect friends. Observe things over time, such as how your trees change. Even if you don't live in a place with seasons, you'll notice changes in the leaves, flowers, and fruits.

▶ Play sensory games outside and inside. What do you hear as you step on dried leaves? What do you smell as a tree starts blooming or the rain starts to fall? How does a tree's bark feel compared with the furry softness of the seeds? What do different fruits, vegetables, and herbs in the garden taste like?

▶ Create a discovery center or table (or even a box, if space is limited) in your classroom, and include different items from nature. Add magnifying glasses and writing and coloring materials so children can make drawings of their observations. Each child can even create their own collection when they go outside and can add it to their individual box or discovery center. They can record what they notice in individual notebooks.

▶ Incorporate natural materials in different learning centers and activities.

- Add twigs to the construction area.

- Weave leaves together (for fine-motor practice).

- Explore the cool feeling of mud in the sensory area. Watch what happens as you keep adding water.

- Press flowers and use them in artwork.

- Do texture rubbings with different items.

- Use natural materials, such as leaves tied together, as paintbrushes.

- Experiment with using the chlorophyll in leaves for color in art.

- Use pebbles as counters.

Put your washing machine to the test. Embrace the dirt and all the joy and learning opportunities nature can bring to you and the children!

Here's some more reading with suggestions for teaching and learning in nature:

Charner, Kathy, Mary B. Rein, and Brittany Roberts, eds. 2012. *Let's Take It Outside! Teacher-Created Activities for Outdoor Learning.* Lewisville, NC: Gryphon House.

Keeler, Rusty. 2008. *Natural Playscapes: Creating Outdoor Play Environments for the Soul.* Lincoln, NE: Exchange Press.

Keeler, Rusty. 2016. *Seasons of Play: Natural Environments of Wonder.* Lewisville, NC: Gryphon House.

Selly, Patty Born. 2017. *Teaching STEM Outdoors: Activities for Young Children.* St. Paul, MN: Redleaf Press.

Dear Family,

Your child will come home filthy sometimes, and we hope you know that means they had a great day! They didn't just dig in the dirt to make the greatest challenge your washing machine has ever seen. They created their own world in which they "cooked" delicious mud pies; tried to catch butterflies and learned just how fast they can fly; stirred leaves together to make soup and then hid treasures underneath; watched how the tree on their regular walk changed over time; and breathed in fresh, energizing air, all while stimulating their physical, emotional, and cognitive development.

Playing and exploring in nature have so many benefits. We know from research that young children who are exposed to more natural environments have improved immune systems. Your children's physical, emotional, and mental health and development are supported with time outdoors. They also develop a love and respect for nature, which will later affect the way they see their role in preserving nature. So get your family outside and enjoy!

Even if you live in an apartment with no park nearby, you can find many ways to enjoy the great outdoors and bring the outside in. The most important thing is to have fun and let your children do the same! Worried about their clothes? Set aside older clothes as their explorer clothes so they (and you) can fully enjoy the experience.

Go for walks and play a noticing game together. What do you see, smell, and hear? You can play this game while you're running errands, waiting in a line, and so on. It will help children to use their senses and support their self-regulation skills by helping them to pause and notice, which is important for concentration and focus.

Let your children explore and just have fun—the more curious they are, the better. When they can try out new things without a specific goal or idea in mind, a world of possibilities opens up. A tree can suddenly become a fort, a safe base for a game of tag, a desert island, or a flag pole. Join them in their play and let them bring you into their world.

Start a little garden with your children. Choose easy-to-grow plants, flowers, herbs, fruits, or vegetables. You can talk about what you notice as the plants are growing, draw pictures, and measure the plants over time. Try experiments such as talking and singing to the plants or playing music to see if the plants grow faster. Add herbs and foods you grow to meals you make together to encourage even the pickiest eater to have a taste!

Talk with your children about different ways they can help the environment, such as by recycling, reusing things, making a small compost bin, buying things with less packaging, and turning off the tap when brushing their teeth. Decide on one thing to try together for at least a week, and talk together about what they noticed. Perhaps they will notice how much food waste they prevented when they added it to the compost bin, or how much water they saved by turning off the tap.

It might sound a little trite, but just stopping to smell the roses can sometimes be the best thing for your children and for you!

Playfully,

*School-to-Home Connections*   Gryphon House

# Chapter 18:
## Behavior Is Communication

Listening and paying attention to children's interests and cues goes beyond developing your classroom experiences. Children can communicate subtly, sometimes in ways that seem disruptive or challenging. By paying attention, you can get to the root of the message a child is trying to convey.

Sometimes children ask for things in the least obvious ways, but if we keep observing, listening, and getting to know them, then we can work with them to find out what they need, even when asking them directly isn't feasible. Most incidents that might be considered "misbehavior" are actually children telling us they have a need that is not being met and they don't know how to get help or ask for what they truly need. As we get to know the children, we'll notice that a baby's cries sound different when hungry or tired. We'll notice how a toddler's smile changes at different times, and we'll pick up on the little indicators signaling when to rush that toddler to the bathroom when potty training.

When I was an assistant teacher, one of our three-year-olds would sporadically act up on the playground, kicking and hitting other children and exhibiting behaviors that would result in him being removed from the playground to calm down. One day as I took him inside, he asked, "Is the garbage truck coming today?" The garbage truck sometimes picked up trash during playtime, and we would all wave and say hello. However, this little boy had recently had ear surgery; the loud sound of the garbage truck was probably too loud and too scary for him. Rather than be near the truck, he preferred to lose playtime and be safe inside. I took him outside and showed him the protective bars around the playground. I explained that no one could come into the playground, that the garbage collector was there to help us keep the school clean and that teachers were there to keep him safe. After that, the random outbursts at playtime stopped.

Sometimes the lightbulb moment doesn't just happen. But you can make notes to figure out the cause, such as by using an antecedent-behavior-consequence (ABC) chart. On an ABC chart, you record the *antecedent* to a behavior—what happened right before something occurred. Next record what the *behavior* was. Then jot down the *consequence* for the behavior. Over time, you can use this information to identify trends.

We might find ourselves in situations we never anticipated, with children asking or talking about deeply personal topics, such as those who are starting to question their gender identity or learning about this as a family member transitions; children whose family situation is changing, such as those going into foster care, welcoming new siblings or parents, or losing loved ones; children whose families have just lost jobs or who have had to suddenly move in with others or into shelters; children whose families have experienced discrimination or whose families have discriminated against their friends and told them they can't play with them anymore because they're different; and children who are facing major illnesses. As little ones try to process such big issues, behavioral challenges might arise, or they may try to express themselves and share with you in different ways. We owe them honest answers that are appropriate for their age and understanding. We also owe them respect when they share things about how they feel, who they are, and who they'd like to become. Children deserve teachers and an environment that celebrates them and helps them to learn about and celebrate others.

You've likely heard some version of the phrase, "Sometimes the children who need the most love ask for it in the most unloving ways," and sighed and thought, "But how much more can I handle?" Children usually exhibit challenging behaviors because a need or want isn't being met, or because they don't know what they should be doing instead. If we approach it from these angles, it can help us to take a softer approach focused on supporting rather than punishing children. Addressing challenging behavior during early childhood can reduce the likelihood of these issues leading to later academic issues, including decreased motivation, problems focusing and persisting with tasks, and continued behavioral challenges (Bulotsky-Shearer et al. 2011; Cipani 1998; Webster-Stratton 1997, as cited in Ritz et al. 2014). Behavioral issues in preschool, such as physical aggression, are also predictive of criminal behavior later in life (Reiss and Roth 2003, as cited in Duncan, Ludwig, and Magnuson 2007). Children aren't "bad," and they're not born destined to be criminals. But if their needs for safety, love, attention, and connection aren't met, and they experience trauma, neglect, or have an underlying physical or mental condition, then behavioral issues can be exacerbated.

Unfortunately, there is no magic wand for addressing challenging behavior, and sometimes change comes so slowly you might not notice at first. You might get home and think, "Wait, there were only two outbursts today not five," or celebrate when a child who used to run screaming around the room when faced with a consequence actually carried out the task instead. Hang in there, keep breathing, and keep sharing the love with the children and yourself.

## Reflect on Your Interpretation and Approach

Before you judge and consider the problems, have you reflected on whether there really is a problem? Could your personal biases, background, experiences, or exhaustion be contributing to how you are interpreting a situation (even if it's subconscious)? Is this a behavior problem or challenge, or is this an issue because of your personal lens? One person's handful could be another's very eager and energetic student. Take some time, breathe, and really think about it.

Expulsion rates in early childhood programs are very troubling. Young children in state-funded preschools have an expulsion rate that is three times higher than those in K–12, and children in private and community preschools have even higher expulsion rates (Gilliam 2005; Gilliam and Shahar 2006; US Department of Education 2016, as cited in Wymer, Williford, and L'hospital 2020). Expulsion doesn't actually solve problems; it only removes children from the very setting where they can learn the skills they need to succeed. Those who are suspended or expelled as young children are more likely to drop out of school, earn less money when working, and become involved in the criminal justice system in later life (Monahan et al. 2014, as cited in Wymer, Williford, and L'hospital 2020; Pascoe and Smart Richman 2009). Even more worrying is that Black children are expelled at twice the rate of White children (US Department of Health and Human Services and Department of Education 2014, as cited in Wymer, Williford, and L'hospital 2020). Research has shown that the higher rate is not due to

Black children displaying more negative behaviors than White children. Are we as teachers doing our part to see, understand, respect, and support all children? Or are our subconscious and conscious biases affecting the way we interpret children's intentions and behaviors (US Department of Health and Human Services and Department of Education 2014, as cited in Wymer, Williford, and L'hospital 2020)?

If you feel too close to a situation to see it, ask a colleague with a different teaching style or approach than yours to come in and observe and brainstorm with you. Be open to what they have to share and to what you find out as you reflect.

## Observe

It can also be difficult for you to notice trends and possible triggers that contribute to challenging behaviors. Create an ABC chart on which you can record your observations. Note the dates and times along with what happened right **before** a challenging behavior occurred, the behavior or response that occurred, and the consequence. Over time, you will begin to see any trends that stand out and can be addressed to minimize triggers. For example, reminding children of what they can do to calm down when they are frustrated or helping them to succeed in the frustrating activity can prevent the challenging behavior.

Think about the little one who acted out to escape the loud garbage truck. The antecedent was the noisy truck, or the fear that the noisy truck was about to arrive. The behavior was kicking and hitting other children. The consequence was the child being taken inside, where he was rewarded by feeling safe from the noisy truck. By showing and explaining to him the safety measures we had in place and the fact that garbage collectors were helping us by taking away our trash, I helped him feel safer and understood. The reason for his challenging behavior was no longer a problem.

## Set Them Up For Success

Set the children up for success by thinking about what they need to be successful. Are components such as your environment, schedule, and approach to teaching and learning working in their favor? For example, if you notice children fidgeting and getting antsy during certain times of the day, could it be that they are expected to sit still for too long? Is it possible that they haven't had enough time to move and play freely? If you notice that children are always asking for your help in a center or getting off task, is it because they have to climb or move things around to reach items that should be easily accessible to them?

Clear, specific, and consistent expectations and instructions can help children know what to do rather than what *not* to do. If you tell me, "Don't run," does that mean I can skip instead, or do I need to walk down the hallway? What does "Be nice" mean? How do I show that? Children must be taught how to use kind words such as *please* and *thank you*, how to share, and how to take turns. Allow children to help you to create the expectations together, so you create a community based on their needs too. Be consistent with expectations and with consequences. If it is particularly difficult to remain consistent and supportive during a long tantrum or episode, you may need to tag team with another colleague. That way, the child always encounters someone who is calm, supportive, and in control. The goal is to focus on strategies that stop the negative behavior, prevent it from recurring, and replace it with appropriate behaviors (Ritz et al. 2014).

## Ignore When Possible

Whenever possible, ignore a behavior—particularly if it is not harming the child or others. Then, try redirecting the child to do something more constructive. Your first priority, however, is to keep all children safe, including the child who might be involved in the episode. Some behaviors will decrease or cease if ignored. If anyone is in danger, then you may need to remove the child from the space and take them to a space where they can't harm themselves or others. As soon as the child is calm and able to, they should return to the group.

## Provide Logical Consequences

Instead of punishment, consider logical consequences. Children need to learn that actions have results; however, they can learn from their mistakes and make things right if something goes wrong. For example, if something gets broken, allow children to try to fix it. If a friend's feelings are hurt, ask them to think of ways they can help their friend to feel better. Note that I didn't say, "Tell him you're sorry." Forcing them to "say sorry" even if they don't mean it only teaches them to use *sorry* as an easy out.

## Create a Community of Care

It's especially important to not only prevent behavioral challenges but also help children to develop strategies to manage their feelings and responses in a constructive manner. Creating a community of care and respect where everyone supports each other and holds each other accountable can help children to feel supported and responsible for each other's well-being. They can help each other by reminding each other of agreed-upon expectations and encouraging each other to use calming strategies when they are upset. This can be more effective than using rewards and bribes to get children to behave, which also teaches them to use external rather than internal motivators.

The community of care extends beyond the classroom to the children's families. When you've already established strong, open relationships with families, discussing an issue that arises will be much smoother because the family will know that you have their child's and their best interests at heart. This can be particularly helpful if you need to recommend to families that their child be referred to specialists for further assessment and support.

Realize that conflict will always arise, even in our own lives. Our role is to help children manage conflict and the feelings that can arise appropriately. We are there to mediate and coach them so they can become independent problem solvers. Helping them to calm down, listen to each other, consider their own and others' feelings, and work together to come up with a solution are important skills (that some adults haven't even mastered yet).

Addressing challenging behavior can be quite taxing for you, so just imagine how taxing it must be for children who are asking for help in their own roundabout way. Take a few deep breaths together and smile, so that both you and the children know that it will all be okay.

The Center on the Social and Emotional Foundations for Early Learning has free resources and tips for teachers and parents including training modules on challenging behavior available at http://csefel.vanderbilt.edu/

Here's some suggested reading if you'd like to learn more:

Bilmes, Jenna. 2012. *Beyond Behavior Management: The Six Life Skills Children Need.* 2nd ed. St. Paul, MN: Redleaf Press.

DeMeo, William. 2013. *When Nothing Else Works: What Early Childhood Professionals Can Do to Reduce Challenging Behaviors.* Lewisville, NC: Gryphon House.

Mitchell, Grace. 1990. *A Very Practical Guide to Discipline with Young Children.* Rev. ed. Owings Mills, MD: Telshare Publishing.

Morhard, Ruth Hanford. 2013. *Wired to Move: Facts and Strategies for Nurturing Boys in an Early Childhood Setting.* Lewisville, NC: Gryphon House.

Sprung, Barbara, Merle Froschl, and Blythe Hinitz. 2005. *The Anti-Bullying and Teasing Book for Preschool Classrooms.* Silver Spring, MD: Gryphon House.

Warner, Laverne, and Sharon A. Lynch. 2004. *Preschool Classroom Management: 150 Teacher-Tested Techniques.* Silver Spring, MD: Gryphon House.

Welch, Ginger. 2019. *How Can I Help? A Teacher's Guide to Early Childhood Behavioral Health.* Lewisville, NC: Gryphon House.

Dear Family,

As a parent, you will probably encounter many challenges managing your own emotions as you try to understand and guide your child's behavior. You and your child can navigate challenges together if you base your approach to behavior management on two things: how to best serve your child, and the understanding that negative behaviors are a child's way of telling you something is wrong or their needs aren't being met. Focus on strategies that stop the unwanted behavior, prevent it from recurring, and replace it with appropriate behaviors.

> ▶ **Set your child up for success.** The goal with behavior management is to prevent problematic behaviors from occurring in the first place. Ask yourself, "What does my child need to be successful?" For example, challenging behaviors frequently occur during transitions from one activity to another. Before transitioning, give your child a heads-up. Five minutes (or longer if you know your child needs more time) before they must stop what they're doing, say, "In five minutes, it'll be time to clean up your toys." Then one minute before, say, "In one minute, it'll be time to clean up your toys." When it's time, get your child started on cleaning up.
>
> If you know your child has a particular challenge doing certain things, such as going to new places, then talk about what will happen, show pictures if you have them, and role-play beforehand. For example, role-play going to the doctor and explain what will happen, or show pictures of new people your child will meet and the house you'll be staying at before your family reunion.
>
> When your child is already calm, practice using calming strategies such as taking deep breaths or dancing. Later, if your child becomes upset, remind them to take deep breaths or invite them to dance with you so that they can calm themselves down.
>
> ▶ **Note trends.** Make notes about recurring behavior to see if you can identify trends that might help you address the underlying issues and support your child. For example, jot down what happened right before the incident, what happened during the incident, and what happened after. Then, when you look through the notes, you might realize that your child's recurring emotional outburst might be a result of fear, hunger, or in response to dreading an event such as nap time in the dark or you leaving for work. Once you know what is triggering the behavior, think about ways you can help your child be successful—you can even

brainstorm together. If, for example, your child often has a tantrum in the afternoon, consider that your child might be overstimulated and tired or hungry. Offer a snack and some quiet time looking at a book together. If your child dreads nap time in the dark, consider adding a cool nightlight to the bedroom.

- **Be calm, clear, and consistent.** Neither you nor your child can have a productive resolution if you're both upset. It's okay to say, "Let's talk when we're both calm." Use calming strategies such as drawing, sipping water slowly, and breathing deeply to help.

  Give clear directions or instructions, such as "Use gentle hands," so your child knows the expected behavior. Saying, "Don't kick your brother," might mean that hitting him instead is okay. Be consistent so your child knows what to expect, and respond accordingly. Your child expects you to follow through with what you are saying, so think carefully before boxing yourself into a corner with a threat you can't follow through on. It's better to wait for you and your child to calm down and discuss things together than it is to escalate a problem with a threat. If you give in to children's screaming demands after five minutes, they will learn that they can outlast you and tomorrow they'll scream for ten minutes instead.

- **Have developmentally appropriate expectations.** Misunderstandings about children's behavior can occur if you expect more from them than they're developmentally ready to do. Toddlers and young children aren't developmentally ready to share, so expecting them to share their special toy with a visiting child without a tantrum is unrealistic. That's understandable if you think about it; even you don't share certain things with everyone. Instead, provide the same materials for each child at a play date.

- **Realistically consider children's attention span.** You can't expect children to sit still at very long events (when you are probably fidgeting too), so plan to take a walk or have a quiet toy to play with to minimize the chances of a tantrum or outburst.

- **Use logical consequences.** Use logical consequences to help your child learn from what happened and find a resolution. For example, if something was broken during a sibling fight or rowdy game, allow them to fix it. Encourage them to help you to think of a solution so it feels authentic to them. Rather than forcing them to say *sorry* to someone when they don't feel very sorry, point out how the person is feeling and

*School-to-Home Connections*  Gryphon House

ask them to think of something they could do to help the person to feel better. For example, say, "I see that your sister is sad. She's crying. What could you do to help her feel better?"

▸ **Get additional help when you need it.** Children's behavioral issues could be indicators of the need for additional support. Don't worry—this doesn't mean you've done something wrong. It just means that your child might need help to heal from trauma, correct chemical imbalances, or to address other physical or mental health needs. Seek help and advice when you need it.

Just as our own temperaments and needs differ from person to person, so do each child's. When things get hard, just keep breathing. We are here to help you too, so keep observing, listening to, and supporting your child, and we'll figure it out together. The Center on the Social and Emotional Foundations for Early Learning has free resources and tips available at http://csefel.vanderbilt.edu/

Here's some additional reading if you'd like to find out more:

Greene, Ross W. 2014. *The Explosive Child: A New Approach for Understanding and Parenting Easily Frustrated, Chronically Inflexible Children.* New York: HarperCollins.

Hargis, Aubrey. 2018. *Toddler Discipline for Every Age and Stage: Effective Strategies to Tame Tantrums, Overcome Challenges, and Help Your Child Grow.* Emeryville, CA: Rockridge Press.

Ockwell-Smith, Sarah. 2017. *Gentle Discipline: Using Emotional Connection— Not Punishment—to Raise Confident, Capable Kids.* New York: TarcherPerigee.

Siegel, Daniel J., and Tina P. Bryson. 2016. *No-Drama Discipline: The Whole-Brain Way to Calm the Chaos and Nurture Your Child's Developing Mind.* New York: Random House.

Warmly,

# Chapter 19:
## How Can I Tell If They're Learning?

You can document young children's learning and progress in lots of ways without succumbing to developmentally inappropriate methods such as tests. If you continue to stay grounded in what's best for the children and in methods that allow their unique abilities and dispositions to shine, then you'll see their growth in a well-rounded manner that leads to a much clearer, holistic picture of the whole child. Stay focused on learning through play as the best method for young children, and find ways to assess their learning that's aligned to that. A test that puts children under pressure to perform isn't aligned with supporting their holistic development in a nurturing, playful way.

Focus on the process, not the product—just as you should in your activities and environment. Observe how children approach tasks and interactions. When you offer children the ability to freely express themselves, rather than cookie-cutter, one-size-fits-most activities, you'll really be able to highlight children's individuality.

## Observe and Document

If you carefully observe children throughout their explorations, conversations, and approaches to challenges, you'll be able to gather evidence of their thinking, learning, and growth. Observing children and taking notes can be particularly important when you are concerned about how a child is progressing and absorbing information. This will help you track progress more clearly and will also provide valuable background information should the child need to be referred for assessments and additional support. You can document evidence of learning in a variety of ways, including the following:

- ▸ Notes, photos, and videos

- ▸ Portfolios

- Classroom displays

- Formative assessment and developmental checklists

## Notes, Photos, and Videos

Take notes and pictures of children as they're working on projects and activities, not just the final product. For example, note short samples of conversations you have with children. Ask open-ended questions, such as the following:

- How do you know?

- Tell me more about . . .

- How did you decide to . . . ?

- Why did you choose . . . ?

- Why do you think that happened?

- What do you think will happen if . . . ?

- How do you think _____ might be feeling? How would you feel if _____?

- What can you do about it?

Take notes of children's responses. You will be surprised by their level of thinking.

Take photos or video of the children as they work, play, and explore. Document children's process during a project or activity by adding descriptions and captions to pictures of children's efforts so that children can be a part of the process. These pictures and videos will help families develop an understanding of their children's approach to tasks and learning.

## Portfolios

Save samples of children's efforts, and date the back (with a sticky note if they don't want you to mark the back) so that you can create a portfolio showing each child's efforts over time. Depending on the child's age and developmental level, you may notice that the child has added more detail and sophistication to illustrations or has progressed from making scribbles to letter-like shapes to letters. Some children may even write words and parts of (or whole) sentences. You may notice that a child who struggled at the beginning of the year to show understanding of some numbers has progressed to understanding numbers up to five or even ten.

## Classroom Displays

Similar to portfolios, collect evidence of children's learning through photos and children's drawings and other artifacts and display these in the classroom. Add descriptions and captions to the displays of children's efforts so that the children can be a part of the process. These displays will help families develop an understanding of their children's learning, and children will be excited to show their families what they have created.

## Formative Assessment and Developmental Checklists

Ensure that you are planning for children's holistic development by monitoring children's development through reference documents, such as developmental checklists and the developmental standards for your area that consider different developmental domains. You might also choose to use formative assessments that are informal or created by you, created by the school with your input, or provided by other organizations. Norm-referenced or "normed" assessments can be helpful when considering how the children are doing when compared to a group, such as the national average or expectation for children's language or physical development by a certain age. Formative assessments can also include targeted teacher observations across developmental domains. Always ensure that the assessment chosen and the way it is carried out are developmentally appropriate and do not cause unnecessary stress to children. Information from checklists or assessments will be especially helpful if you are monitoring children's development in case they need to be referred for additional support.

Depending on the educational system you are in, the parents and teachers in other grades might expect a report card outlining different areas of children's development. Ensure that the report is developmentally appropriate and covers all areas of children's development, including physical and social-emotional areas, not just the academic areas. Thoughtful comments and anecdotal information are particularly important to help parents and families to learn more about their child.

Share the documentation, observations, and assessments with families, and use these artifacts and data as springboards for further communication and connection. You can post documentation and examples of children's efforts in locations that are visible to parents at drop-off and pickup times and share pictures using social media or specific group chats on phones. Consider hosting family nights and events, and have one-on-one consultations with each family a few times per year. A strong relationship between you and the families will not only benefit the children you serve with love but also make your job much easier in the long run.

Here's a little more reading if you'd like to explore assessments further:

Bredekamp, Sue. 2019. *Effective Practices in Early Childhood Education: Building a Foundation.* 4th ed. Carmel, IN: Pearson Education.

Featherstone, Sally, ed. 2013. *Catching Them at It! Assessment in the Early Years.* Rev. ed. London, UK: Featherstone Education, Ltd.

Grace, Cathy, and Elizabeth Shores. 1998. *The Portfolio Book: A Step-By-Step Guide for Teachers.* Silver Spring, MD: Gryphon House.

Here's some suggested reading for your inclusive classroom:

Cook, Ruth, M. Diane Klein, and Deborah Chen. 2019. *Adapting Early Childhood Curricula for Children with Disabilities and Special Needs.* 10th ed. Carmel, IN: Pearson Education.

Gould, Patti, and Joyce Sullivan. 1999. *The Inclusive Early Childhood Classroom: Easy Ways to Adapt Learning Centers for All Children.* Silver Spring, MD: Gryphon House.

Lynch, Sharon, Diana Nabors, Cynthia Simpson, and Laverne Warner. 2008. *Themes for Inclusive Classrooms: Lesson Plans for Every Learner.* Silver Spring, MD: Gryphon House.

Schiller, Pam, and Clarissa Willis. 2008. *Inclusive Literacy Lessons for Early Childhood.* Silver Spring, MD: Gryphon House.

Shelton, Tricia, and Mary Renck Jalongo. 2016. *Practical Strategies for Supporting Young Learners with Autism Spectrum Disorder.* Lewisville, NC: Gryphon House.

Smutny, Joan F., Sally Y. Walker, and Ellen Honeck. 2015. *Teaching Gifted Children in Today's Preschool and Primary Classrooms: Identifying, Nurturing, and Challenging Children Ages 4–9.* Golden Valley, MN: Free Spirit.

Warner, Laverne, Sharon Lynch, Diana Nabors, and Cynthia Simpson. 2007. *Inclusive Lesson Plans throughout the Year.* Silver Spring, MD: Gryphon House.

Wilmot, Keriann. 2020. *Wired Differently: A Teacher's Guide to Understanding Sensory Processing Challenges.* Lewisville, NC: Gryphon House.

Dear Family,

Many of us will think back to our own early schooling experiences and remember break time or recess, lunch, and work time. Work time probably involved writing. These memories might naturally shape what you think of as "school" when you try to gauge whether your child is learning. It's sometimes especially hard to see that they're learning because they're so young. You might be concerned about your child's readiness to transition from preschool and, therefore, you might be tempted to ask about homework and to see what your preschooler is writing.

Keep in mind that at this age *everything* is a learning experience! Educators and researchers have discovered so much about how children learn and the best ways to help them learn. For example, we now know that writing before they're ready and doing homework at such a young age can negatively affect their love of learning. Consequently, today's preschool experience looks quite different from our own. Nevertheless, you want to know how your child is doing and whether or not they are learning what they need to know to be ready for school. Here are some more authentic ways to check:

- ▶ **Talk with your children**. It really is as simple as that! As you converse with your them and ask follow-up questions, you'll help both their language and thinking skills to develop. You'll hear how their speech is getting more complex—they're adding more words, staying on topic longer, and making more eye contact as you talk. You'll also hear about the things they're learning, about their friends, about their concerns—you name it, it will come out! Even nonverbal children benefit just as much, if not more, from conversations with you. They will babble in response or try to repeat common words you say and will try to stay engaged in the conversation and keep your eye contact for longer. You'll notice changes in their gestures and emotions that indicate their preferences and engagement as well.

- ▶ **Play with your children.** You're probably tired of hearing this by now, but play's the thing! As you play with your children, over time you'll see how their play changes. You'll see how much growth has occurred and will be able to honor their efforts. As babies and toddlers get older, you'll notice that they'll start playing with other children rather than just beside them or watching them from afar. Three- or four-year olds will develop more elaborate building skills and sophisticated role-play games. They might remain engaged or focused on one game or activity for longer periods. They'll begin to want to incorporate "writing" in their planning and artwork, so be sure to include paper and writing tools and encourage their scribbles.

▸ **Talk with us.** Communicate with us regularly. Sign up for special one-on-one conversations that might not be possible during drop-off and pickup. We are here to support you and your children. The information we can offer will give you ways to support your children's learning, growth, and development. This might include a suggestion that children be referred for special services or assessments to see if they require additional support. While this might seem worrying, the earlier children receive support, the easier it will be to help them thrive.

▸ **Celebrate your children's efforts.** Without becoming a hoarder, save some of your children's creations they've made. You can even put a date on the back (ask their permission first or use a sticky note). Compare different examples so that you can see how much more detail they add to their work over time. Take pictures of things you've made together too. We might also save a portfolio to review with you during our consultations, or we may share pictures and documentation of class events and projects.

When you embrace and enjoy all of the moments you have with your children, you'll be able to see how they're blossoming and growing from what might have just seemed like play. If you'd like to learn more about assessments and early intervention for children who might have developmental delays, you can check out *Does My Child Have a Developmental Delay? A Step-by-Step Guide for Parents on Early Intervention* by Sarah Taylor Vanover.

Warmly,

*School-to-Home Connections* Gryphon House

# Chapter 20:
## Handling Difficult Situations and Topics with Care

As teachers, you are a part of the children's families and inner circles. They trust you to help them understand and navigate the world, which, unfortunately, is sometimes a scary and traumatic place. Children will tell you about major family events such as illnesses and deaths in the family, or you will see them process events through play. You may also be one of the few people outside a child's family who sees that child on a regular basis. You may notice signs that the child is experiencing abuse or neglect. You are mandated to report your suspicions about a child who might be abused or neglected. While this can be one of the most difficult aspects of your role, the trust the children have in you means that it is also one of the greatest honors of your role as well. Here are some ways you can create a caring, trusting environment where you can communicate with children about difficult topics and situations and support them.

## Communicate with Families

Creating a nurturing environment where children and families feel that they can trust you enough to share with you and ask hard questions begins by setting expectations about respect with families and children. Before the school year starts, create respectful policies for the people in your learning environment, so that families understand that all people and families should be treated with respect. Share these policies with families and children.

Think about the ways respect will be demonstrated in your classroom. For example, intentionally display artifacts and photos and teach children about different cultures, races, celebrations, genders, identities, and families. Children can brainstorm additional expectations with you and can create posters and stories to remind each other and demonstrate how they can respect others and be kind.

Ask families to tell you about anything for which their child might require additional support, such as a severe illness, separation, or recent death in the family. Work with families to agree upon a consistent approach to talking about and supporting their child around this issue and reassure them that you will keep personal information private.

## Reflect

Reflect on the words you use, your tone, and your body language when talking about different people or groups. Do you subconsciously or consciously use words that are derogatory against others? Are the stories and images children see stereotyping persons? Do the stories and images reflect the abilities and potential of all people? Do you pick specific children for certain roles? Do you react more sharply to some more than others? Do you assume that other children might not be able to do certain tasks and assign them different roles based on this? If you're not sure or would like to learn more, ask a colleague to visit and observe the classroom. Or set up a video camera to record different parts of the day over a few days. Are there any trends you notice?

## Be Honest

Start by asking the children what they know about a particular topic first, particularly if they've come to you with questions or you've heard them discussing this among themselves. This will also help you to address any misconceptions they may have and to understand how much detail you might need to provide. Be honest as you speak with children but provide an appropriate amount of information for their developmental and personal needs, so that they are not burdened or frightened with excessive information.

Young children need enough information to understand how this particular issue affects them, their family and friends, and how they can stay safe and healthy. For example, when talking about the COVID-19 pandemic, you might say that a virus like a very bad flu is making people very, very sick, and that you can stay safe by washing your hands, staying home more, and wearing masks. If children have encountered loss, you can say that some people might die and then provide a safe space for children to talk about their losses.

If you're not sure how to tackle a topic, ask for help. Invite a counselor or resource person to visit and share with them. You can even help the children to come up with questions they'd like to ask beforehand.

## Learn Together in a Safe Space

Create a safe space and time for sharing whatever is on children's minds, and model for them how to respect each other's opinions and feelings, even if they disagree. Observe and listen to children throughout the day to learn what they're talking about and what their body language is telling you about these conversations so you can find appropriate ways to support them. Read stories and do projects together to learn more about important people and events. Ask families and community members to share about their culture with the other children.

With your littles, brainstorm ways that you can help or contribute to a solution. They can help write letters to politicians, teach children in other classes about the situation, reduce their waste and recycle to help the environment, talk about ways they can respect others and celebrate differences, and share or donate the things they have if they have more than others.

The best (and sometimes most challenging) thing about working with young children is their straightforward and honest approach to life. If a child blurts out something such as, "My mama says my daddy is a cheating dog," acknowledge what the child said and, if you are in a whole-group setting, provide a response that will help all children process that information. Then follow-up with the child privately to attend to their feelings and needs. For example, in the whole group you can say, "Your mama was probably very mad or hurt about something that your daddy did. Grown-ups have strong feelings and sometimes make mistakes too, just like we do, but they will still take care of you and love you." After, check in with the child privately to see how they're feeling and learn if there are further implications of this phrase, such as the child's parents are separating. Find a time to talk with the family about what the child shared so that they can address it in a loving way at home.

Some children might find it particularly difficult to process loss and will need support as they grieve for loved ones whom they might also have seen declining in health. They might want to speak with you about noticing how a loved one's appearance has changed over time and what happens to a person when they pass away. Talk with parents about how they have been speaking with their child so that you can approach the conversation in a similar way.

Children also process most of what is going on in their life and what they see around them through play, which is why play is so important. Many of the children at a preschool I worked at in Washington, DC, used to pretend to drive to the mall or the liquor store and would pretend to fix teachers a "Jack and Coke," modifying the center's props for use with their main interests. As with our approach to everything the children said, we honored their experiences and what they shared through play, and we "purchased" more child-friendly items as we accompanied them on their pretend trips. We also continued to observe to see if there were any further implications to or concerns about what they were sharing. Although you might feel awkward and uncomfortable, prioritize children's safety and needs when thinking about handling a difficult situation or talking about a difficult topic. Be sure to seek help or report concerns to the relevant agencies.

For additional information on how to support children, here's some suggested reading:

Grace, Cathy, and Elizabeth F. Shores. 2010. *After the Crisis: Using Storybooks to Help Children Cope.* Lewisville, NC: Gryphon House.

Iruka, Iheoma, Stephanie Curenton, Kerry-Ann Escayg, and Tonia Durden. 2020. *Don't Look Away: Embracing Anti-Bias Classrooms.* Lewisville, NC: Gryphon House.

Miller, Karen. 1996. *The Crisis Manual for Early Childhood Teachers: How to Handle the Really Difficult Problems.* Silver Spring, MD: Gryphon House.

Nicholson, Julie, Linda Perez, and Julie Kurtz. 2018. *Trauma-Informed Practices for Early Childhood Educators: Relationship-Based Approaches that Support Healing and Build Resilience in Young Children.* New York: Routledge.

Peterson, Karen. 2014. *Helping Them Heal: How Teachers Can Support Young Children Who Experience Stress and Trauma.* Lewisville, NC: Gryphon House.

Sorrels, Barbara. 2015. *Reaching and Teaching Children Exposed to Trauma.* Lewisville, NC: Gryphon House.

Welch, Ginger, Laura Wilhelm, and Heather Johnson. 2013. *The Neglected Child: How to Recognize, Respond, and Prevent.* Lewisville, NC: Gryphon House.

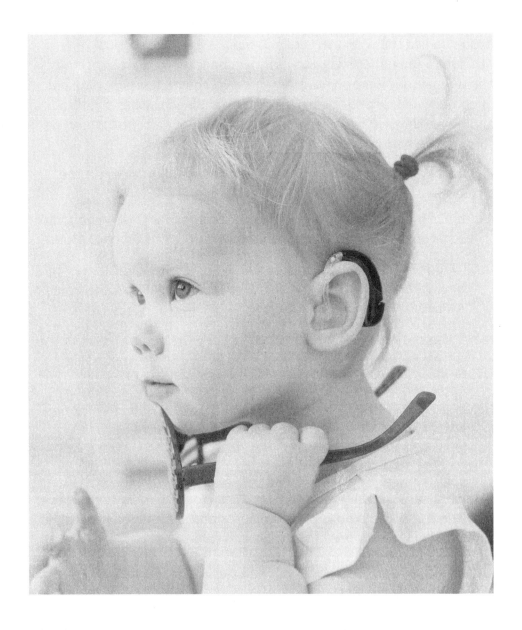

Dear Family,

These are difficult times to be a grown-up as well as to be a parent to a young child. You might be struggling to understand complicated, difficult, inexplicable, or inexcusable issues such as systemic racism, prejudice, and violence against others; the COVID-19 pandemic; or challenging occurrences such as serious illness and death. How do you handle the situation and explain it to a young child who has valid questions and deserves valid answers? Here are some ways to approach difficult subjects with young children.

**First, start with yourself.** Before you start a conversation with young children about a topic such as racism or discrimination, consider how your own biases might be affecting them and what they might be teaching them. You are your children's biggest role model, and they look to you for guidance about how to treat others and how they deserve to be treated. Reflect on the words you use, your tone, and your body language. Do you subconsciously or consciously use words that are derogatory against others? Do you bristle or clutch your things when people of a different race or gender walk past? Do the images they see on the screen stereotype others? Your children pick up on every cue and, if your words don't match your actions, they will ask you about that discrepancy.

**Be honest.** Ask what they already know about a particular topic first, particularly if they've come to you with questions. This will help you to clear up any misconceptions they may have. Talk with your children honestly but at their level. Young children do not need all of the details that might frighten them. They need information to help them understand how an issue or situation affects them, their family, and their friends, and how all of you can stay safe and healthy. For example, when talking about the COVID-19 pandemic, you might have told your children that something like a very bad flu is making people sick. You may have said that you can stay safe by washing your hands, staying home more, and wearing masks. Or, when explaining to your children about child abuse, you might tell them about secret touches and that they should tell you if anyone touches them and says it's a secret and they shouldn't tell anyone. But your children might have questions you haven't thought of or don't know the answer to. It's okay to say, "I don't know. Let's find out together," and then do just that.

If something has happened in your family, such as a conflict your child has witnessed or a separation caused by an indiscretion or deceptions, talk honestly with your child about what happened in a way that's appropriate for the child's age. Remember, the child doesn't need all the details. It's okay to admit that grown-ups make mistakes and sometimes grown-ups get angry or do things they shouldn't. If violence was involved, be very clear that the violence was not okay. Talk through other ways that the situation could have been handled.

Reassure your children that the difficult situation is not their fault and that someone will always love and take care of them. (This is particularly important if the situation has resulted in the child being separated from a key family member.)

**Use stories and books to help children understand what is happening through the characters.** Stories can help them to identify with a character. You can use them as a great conversation starter as your children share how they feel about a similar situation, such as when a family member or pet dies. Books are also a great way to learn about important figures and their history when teaching about discrimination and why we should respect others.

Children can also write their own stories and draw to help them process what is happening, particularly as they process difficult tragedies and trauma. They can draw pictures of what happened, how they're feeling, and what they can do to feel better or stay safe. You can find children's books at your local library. Also, we can recommend some children's books that children may enjoy.

**Honor your children's feelings.** Ask your children how they're feeling, and respect those feelings as you talk with them. Explain that it's okay to have strong feelings, and sometimes we can all feel sad, angry, confused, frustrated, scared, or worried. Ask them about what they need to feel better, and try to reassure them and explain that you are there to keep them safe as you do the suggested things together. If you can't do what your child asks for, such as release a loved one from prison, explain what you *can* do instead, such as draw a picture and write a note to send to the loved one.

**Find ways to help together.** Your children will probably ask about what they can do to help or stay safe. Brainstorm simple child-friendly things that you can do together, such as staying home when you're feeling sick so you don't spread germs, signing petitions or writing letters to politicians about climate change or discriminatory policies, donating items they don't use anymore to a shelter, or being kind and respectful to everyone and encouraging others to do the same.

**Get help if you need it.** If your child or your family has faced trauma or tragedy and needs help to process and heal from it, get help. Just like some illnesses need to be treated with professional help, so do some mental health concerns. There's no shame in it. Lots of counseling opportunities exist, which can make a world of difference.

As long as you approach a difficult situation or topic with love and care, you and your child will be able to get through it together.

Warmly,

*School-to-Home Connections*    Gryphon House

# Chapter 21:
## Transitioning to a New Class or School

Before you know it, the time will come for the children you care for to move on to a new class or school. You can help this transition be as smooth as possible by encouraging them and getting them excited about things to come. Warning them about the extra work and responsibilities they might have as "big kids" will only scare and worry them and could turn them off from transitioning.

Even very young children know what they like and need and can help in the decision-making. At the preschool I used to run, one of the children came for a week because his actual school closed for holidays before ours did, and he also attended our after-care program. After two days at our school, he went home and said, "I'm not going back to [old school]. I go to [new school] now."

## Talk about It

Acknowledge and talk about the children's feelings and understanding about going to a new school. This will also help you clarify any misunderstandings and help them process any fears they may have. Create a class project about things children are excited to do in their new school or class.

## Collaborate with Colleagues

If children are transitioning to another class within the same school or building, share objective information with the new teachers that will help children adjust more easily and allow teachers to get to know the children. Share just enough information for them to make a welcoming environment, without your own biases influencing teachers' opinions about the children before they get a chance to get to know them. For example, share information about children's favorite activities, foods they like/dislike, triggers that might upset them, and helpful strategies to help children get comfortable and participate.

Ask teachers about their expectations for children entering their classes, so that you can help prepare the children for these expectations, such as supporting the development of their self-help skills. If some of the expectations are not developmentally appropriate, talk about your concerns with the teachers.

Ask the teachers and some of the children in that grade to visit with the children in your class to talk about all of the exciting things they'll do. Set up a time for your students to visit their new classrooms too. If the children will stay within the same school or building, visit them after they've transitioned to help them understand that you'll still always be there to support them.

## Collaborate with Families

Talk with the parents in a group or during individual consultations to give them advice about the types of programming that might serve their children best. Provide them with information and documentation about the school selection and transition process in your area. If children are moving on to a new class within the same school, invite the teachers to visit and talk about what they'll be doing to put parents at ease.

Seeing the children you've so lovingly cared for transition to a new classroom or school can be a hard time for early educators. You may not know what will happen to the little personalities you've had the honor to watch emerge. Trust in all of the work you've done to give them a strong foundation and set them on the right path.

Dear Family,

Transitioning out of preschool, whether to a new class or a new school, can be both exciting and stressful for you and your child. If you have school choice, talk with your child about the type of school or class they like. Even if you don't have school choice, ask your child how they're feeling about going to a new school or class. Respect these feelings and reassure your child. Avoid telling them about how hard it will be or about doing lots of work because this could frighten your child and negatively affect the transition process.

Start the school transition process early, and talk with your child's current teachers to see if they have suggestions or advice about a school they would recommend or that would best suit your child and personality, approach to learning, and needs. Set up visits or calls at potential schools, and ask questions that will help you get a feel for the school culture and the approach to teaching and learning there. When you've narrowed down your choices, allow your child to visit the school too to see what they think.

If school choice isn't available where you live, you can still ask questions and request that your child visit for a tour a little before school starts, so that they'll be familiar with the space and you can talk about it together. Ask questions such as:

- Can you give me a sample daily schedule?

- What is your approach to homework?

- What are your expectations for children entering this grade or school?

- What is your discipline policy?

When touring, be sure to take time to just listen and get a feel for the atmosphere and environment. What do the learning environments look and feel like to you? Trust your gut and instincts.

If your child is transitioning to a new class at the same school, ask if you and your child can visit the new class and teacher beforehand, if your child is not familiar with the teacher and the environment. Talk with parents of children attending the schools you are considering. You can also ask the parents if you and your child can talk with their children to ask what they think about their school.

Before your child begins attending the new school or joins the new class, help them to adjust to the new routine by anticipating challenges and practicing beforehand. You can talk about and then role-play different scenarios your child might encounter and find particularly challenging, such as riding a school bus, meeting new classmates and the new teacher, and asking for help. If your child is old enough and doesn't already know, help them to learn their full name, address, your name, and your number in case of emergencies.

On the first day of school, it might be tempting to drop your child off and sneak away while they're distracted or having fun, but it's always important to say goodbye and that you will come back soon. Your child will be much more distressed when they look around for you and you're gone.

At the end of the day, talk with your child about their day and how they're feeling. It's perfectly natural for your child to have a great first few days or week and then resist returning after the weekend when the novelty has worn off. Just keep listening and reassuring them by helping them to problem solve any issues they bring up and addressing major concerns or worries if they arise. Just keep breathing and have no fear—your child (and you) will be just fine! Everything you and your child are now accustomed to started out as something new.

Warmly,

*School-to-Home Connections*   Gryphon House

# Appendix: Children's Books Related to Different Topics

## Behavior Is Communication

Agassi, Martine. 2002. *Hands Are Not for Hitting*. Minneapolis, MN: Free Spirit.

Cole, Elizabeth. 2020. *I Am Stronger than Anger*. Elizabeth Cole.

Cook, Julia. 2005. *My Mouth Is a Volcano!* Chattanooga, TN: National Center for Youth Issues.

Green, Andi. 2020. *The Very Frustrated Monster*. Jersey City, NJ: Monsters in My Head.

Herman, Steve. 2018. *Train Your Angry Dragon*. Tallahassee, FL: DG Books.

Herman, Steve. 2018. *Train Your Dragon to Accept NO*. Tallahassee, FL: DG Books.

Javernick, Ellen. 2010. *What If Everybody Did That?* Tarrytown, NY: Pinwheel Books.

Willems, Mo. 2014. *Waiting Is Not Easy!* New York: Hyperion Books for Children.

## Creating a Child-Centered Environment Where Children Thrive

Olsen, Shannon. 2020. *Our Class Is a Family*. Orange County, CA: Shannon Olsen.

Olsen, Shannon. 2021. *A Letter from Your Teacher on the First Day of School*. Orange County, CA: Shannon Olsen.

## Embracing and Celebrating Our Diverse and Beautiful World

Beer, Sophie. 2018. *Love Makes a Family*. New York: Dial Books for Young Readers.

Harris, C. M. 2019. *What if We Were All the Same!* Orange, CA: Purple Diamond Press.

Katz, Karen. 2002. *The Colors of Us*. New York: Henry Holt and Company.

Kostecki-Shaw, Jenny Sue. 2011. *Same, Same but Different*. New York: Henry Holt and Company.

Leannah, Michael. 2017. *Most People*. Thomaston, ME: Tilbury House.

Palacio, R. J. 2017. *We're All Wonders*. New York: Alfred A. Knopf.

Penfold, Alexandra. 2018. *All Are Welcome*. New York: Penguin.

Purtill, Sharon. 2019. *It's OK to Be Different*. Windsor, ON: Dunhill Clare Publishing.

Sotomayor, Sonia. 2019. *Just Ask! Be Different, Be Brave, Be You.* New York: Philomel.

Sriram, Meera. 2020. *A Gift for Amma: Market Day in India*. Cambridge, MA: Barefoot Books.

## Encouraging Children's Individuality and Uniqueness

Acosta, Alicia, and Luis Amavisca. 2019. *I Love My Colorful Nails*. Boston, MA: NubeOcho Press.

Andreae, Giles. 2012. *Giraffes Can't Dance.* New York: Cartwheel Books.

Avis, Heather. 2021. *Different—A Great Thing to Be!* New York: WaterBrook.

Beaumont, Karen. 2004. *I Like Myself!* Orlando, FL: Harcourt.

Carlson, Nancy. 1990. *I Like Me!* New York: Puffin.

Grabois Fischer, Lauren. 2015. *Be Who You Were Meant to Be*. BE Books.

McKee, David. 1989. *Elmer*. New York: Lothrop, Lee, and Shepard.

Moradian, Afsaneh. 2018. *Jamie Is Jamie: A Book about Being Yourself and Playing Your Way.* Minneapolis, MN: Free Spirit.

O'Hair, Margaret, and Sofia Sanchez. 2021. *You Are Enough: A Book about Inclusion.* New York: Scholastic.

Parr, Todd. 2009. *It's Okay to Be Different*. New York: Little, Brown.

Pearlman, Robb. *Pink Is for Boys*. Philadelphia, PA: Running Press Kids.

Reynolds, Peter H. 2020. *Be You!* New York: Orchard Books.

Thorn, Theresa. 2019. *It Feels Good to Be Yourself: A Book about Gender Identity*. New York: Henry Holt and Company.

## Fine-Motor Development and Writing

Alber, Diane. 2018. *I'm Not Just a Scribble*. Gilbert, AZ: Diane Alber Art.

Alber, Diane. 2019. *Scribble Stones*. Gilbert, AZ: Diane Alber Art.

Daywalt, Drew. 2013. *The Day the Crayons Quit*. New York: Philomel.

Hanlon, Abby. 2012. *Ralph Tells a Story*. Las Vegas, NV: Amazon Children's Publishing.

Johnson, Crockett. 1955/1983. *Harold and the Purple Crayon*. New York: HarperCollins.

Reynolds, Peter H. 2004. *Ish*. Somerville, MA: Candlewick.

## General Encouragement

Estrada, Elizabeth. 2021. *I Choose to Speak Up*. Elizabeth Estrada.

Marley, Bob, and Cedella Marley. 2012. *Every Little Thing*. San Francisco: Chronicle Books.

Paul, Miranda. 2020. *Speak Up*. Boston, MA: Clarion Books.

Reynolds, Peter H. 2019. *Say Something!* New York: Orchard Books.

## Grief and Loss

Herman, Steve. 2019. *The Sad Dragon*. Tallahassee, FL: DG Books

Karst, Patrice. 2018. *The Invisible String*. New York: Little, Brown.

Lambert-Prater, Tracy. 2020. *Why Do I Feel So Sad?* Emeryville, CA: Rockridge Press.

## Intentional Interactions and the Power of *Yet*

Ferguson, Fabian E. 2020. *Jackie Wins Them All*. Newark, NJ: F. Ferguson Books.

Garcia, Gabi. 2018. *I Can Do Hard Things: Mindful Affirmations for Kids*. Austin, TX: Skinned Knee Publishing.

Herman, Steve. 2020. *Train Your Dragon to Do Hard Things*. Tallahassee, FL: DG Books.

Kenney, Daniel. 2018. *I Am Not Afraid to Fail*. Trendwood Press.

Kenney, Daniel. 2018. *I Won't Give Up*. Trendwood Press.

Krauss, Ruth. 1945. *The Carrot Seed.* New York: Harper and Row.

Lionni, Leo. 1995. *Matthew's Dream*. New York: Dragonfly Books.

Piper, Watty. 1930. *The Little Engine That Could*. New York: Platt and Munk.

Reynolds, Peter H. 2003. *The Dot*. Somerville, MA: Candlewick.

Willems, Mo. 2010. *Can I Play Too?* New York: Hyperion Books for Children.

Williams, Vera B. 1982. *A Chair for My Mother*. New York: Greenwillow.

Wilson, Kiara. 2021. *Mistakes Are How I Learn*. Amazing Affirmations.

Wright, Laurie. 2018. *I Will Try*. Laurie Wright.

## Involving Infants

Arena, Jen. 2014. *Besos for Baby: A Little Book of Kisses*. New York: LB Kids.

Becker, Aaron. 2019. *You Are Light*. Somerville, MA: Candlewick.

Boynton, Sandra. 1982. *Moo, Baa, La La La!* New York: Little Simon.

Brown, Margaret Wise. 1947. *Goodnight Moon*. New York: Harper and Row.

Campbell, Rod. 2007. *Dear Zoo: A Lift-the-Flap Book*. New York: Little Simon.

Cousins, Lucy. 2018. *Where Is Little Fish?* Somerville, MA: Candlewick.

DuoPress. 2017. *Hello, Baby Animals: A High-Contrast Book*. Baltimore, MD: DuoPress.

Frost, Maddie. 2018. *Hello, Farm!* Indestructible series. New York: Workman Publishing. (The Indestructibles series of books are washable, chewable, and rip-proof.)

Global Fund for Children. 2007. *Global Babies*. Watertown, MA: Charlesbridge.

Hepworth, Amelia. 2015. *I Love You to the Moon and Back*. Wilton, CT: Tiger Tales.

Kashiwara, Akio. 2018. *Baby Sees Colors! A Totally Mesmerizing High-Contrast Book for Babies*. New York: Gakken.

### Language and Literacy

Ho, Mingfong. 1996. *Hush! A Thai Lullaby*. New York: Orchard Books.

Kontis, Alethea. 2012. *AlphaOops! The Day Z Went First*. Somerville, MA: Candlewick.

Lewis, Kevin. 2002. *My Truck Is Stuck!* New York: Hyperion Books for Children.

Martin, Bill Jr., and John Archambault. 2000. *Chicka Chicka Boom Boom*. New York: Beach Lane Books.

McGregor, Leesa. 2021. *A New Alphabet for Humanity*. Glasgow, Scotland, UK: Impact Humanity Publishing.

Rinker, Sherri D. 2011. *Goodnight, Goodnight, Construction Site*. San Francisco: Chronicle Books.

Shannon, David. 1998. *No, David!* New York: Scholastic.

Wood, Audrey. 1999. *Silly Sally*. New York: Red Wagon.

Wood, Audrey. 2009. *The Napping House*. Boston, MA: Houghton Mifflin Harcourt.

## Nurturing in Nature

Dr. Seuss. 1971. *The Lorax*. New York: Random House.

Ferland, Lisa. 2020. *We Walk through the Forest*. Åkersberga, Swed.: Lisa Ferland.

Oxenbury, Helen. 1996. *We're Going on a Bear Hunt*. London, UK: Walker Books.

Parr, Todd. 2010. *The Earth Book*. New York: Little, Brown.

Teckentrup, Britta. 2016. *Tree: A Peek-Through Picture Book*. New York: Doubleday.

## Physical Development

Carle, Eric. 1997. *From Head to Toe*. New York: HarperCollins.

Child, Lauren. 2000. *I Will Never Not Ever Eat a Tomato*. Somerville, MA: Candlewick.

Ehlert, Lois. 1996. *Eating the Alphabet*. New York: Red Wagon.

Ehlert, Lois. 1987. *Growing Vegetable Soup*. New York: Harcourt.

Hicks, Barbara Jean. 2009. *Monsters Don't Eat Broccoli*. New York: Dragonfly.

Mitton, Tony. 2002. *Dinosaurumpus!* New York: Scholastic.

Pryor, Katherine. 2012. *Sylvie's Spinach*. San Francisco: Readers to Eaters.

Rockwell, Lizzy. 2004. *The Busy Body Book: A Kid's Guide to Fitness*. New York: Alfred A. Knopf.

Schofield-Morrison, Connie. 2014. *I Got the Rhythm*. New York: Bloomsbury.

## Race and Racism

Chung, Aree. 2018. *Mixed: A Colorful Story*. New York: MacMillan.

Harris, C. M. 2019. *What If We Were All the Same!* Orange, CA: Purple Diamond Press.

Herman, Steve. 2019. *Teach Your Dragon about Diversity*. Tallahassee, FL: DG Books

Kates, Bobbi. 1992. *We're Different, We're the Same*. New York: Random House.

Madison, Megan, and Jessica Ralli. 2021. *Our Skin: A First Conversation about Race*. New York: Rise x Penguin Workshop.

## Safety

Herman, Steve. 2019. *Teach Your Dragon about Stranger Danger*. Tallahassee, FL: DG Books.

Herman, Steve. 2021. *Teach Your Dragon Body Safety*. Tallahassee, FL: DG Books.

Sanders, Jayneen. 2016. *My Body! What I Say Goes!* Victoria, Aus.: Upload Publishing.

## Separation

Abercrombie, Barbara. 1995. *Charlie Anderson*. New York: Aladdin Books.

Herman, Steve. 2020. *Two Homes Filled with Love*. Tallahassee, FL: DG Books.

## STEM for Young Children

Beaty, Andrea. 2007. *Iggy Peck, Architect*. New York: Abrams Books for Young Readers.

Beaty, Andrea. 2013. *Rosie Revere, Engineer*. New York: Abrams Books for Young Readers.

Beaty, Andrea. 2016. *Ada Twist, Scientist*. New York: Abrams Books for Young Readers.

Berkes, Marianne. 2004. *Over in the Ocean: In a Coral Reef*. Nevada City, CA: Dawn Publications.

Christelow, Eileen. 2006. *Five Little Monkeys Jumping on the Bed*. Boston, MA: Clarion Books.

Cornwall, Gaia. 2020. *Jabari Tries*. Somerville, MA: Candlewick.

Gonzalez, Maya Christina. 2013. *My Colors, My World/mis colores, mi mundo*. New York: Lee and Low.

Krebs, Laurie. 2017. *We All Went on Safari: A Counting Journey through Tanzania*. Cambridge, MA: Barefoot Books.

Litwin, Eric. 2010. *Pete the Cat: I Love My White Shoes*. New York: Harper.

Portis, Antoinette. 2006. *Not a Box*. New York: HarperCollins.

Portis, Antoinette. 2007. *Not a Stick*. New York: HarperCollins.

Thong, Roseanne Greenfield. 2013. *Round Is a Tortilla: A Book of Shapes*. San Francisco: Chronicle Books.

Yamada, Kobi. 2014. *What Do You Do with an Idea?* Tuart Hill, Western Aus.: Compendium.

Yolen, Jane. 2004. *How Do Dinosaurs Count to Ten?* New York: Blue Sky Press.

## Supporting Social-Emotional Development

Diesen, Deborah. 2021. *The Pout-Pout Fish and the Mad, Mad Day*. New York: Farrar, Straus, and Giroux.

Estrada, Elizabeth. 2021. *I Choose to Calm My Anger*. Elizabeth Estrada.

Garcia, Gabi. 2017. *Listening with My Heart: A Story of Kindness and Self-Compassion*. Austin, TX: Skinned Knee Publishing.

Green, Andi. 2009. *The Monster in the Bubble: A Children's Book about Change*. Jersey City, NJ: Monsters in My Head.

Green, Andi. 2011. *Don't Feed the WorryBug: A Children's Book about Worry*. Jersey City, NJ: Monsters in My Head.

Herman, Steve. 2018. *Help Your Dragon Deal with Anxiety*. Tallahassee, FL: DG Books.

Herman, Steve. 2018. *The Mindful Dragon: A Dragon Book about Mindfulness*. Tallahassee, FL: DG Books.

James, LeBron. 2020. *I Promise*. New York: HarperCollins.

McCloud, Carol. 2006/2016. *Have You Filled a Bucket Today? A Guide to Daily Happiness for Kids*. Brighton, MI: Bucket Philosophy.

O'Sullivan, Cathryn. 2021. *I Have Feelings.* Kingston, Jamaica: Caribbean Child Development Centre, The University of the West Indies Open Campus, and DoGood Jamaica. (This is a free book that can be accessed at http://bit.ly/ihavefeelings)

Verde, Susan. 2018. *I Am Human: A Book of Empathy*. New York: Abrams Books for Young Readers.

Wright, Laurie. 2018. *I Believe in Myself*. Laurie Wright.

Yamada, Kobi. 2016. *What Do You Do with a Problem?* Tuart Hill, Western Aus.: Compendium.

### Terrific Toddlers

Carle, Eric. 1994. *The Very Hungry Caterpillar.* New York: Philomel.

Knapp, Andrew. 2017. *Let's Find Momo! A Hide-and-Seek Board Book.* Philadelphia, PA: Quirk Books.

Kubler, Annie. 2009. *Head, Shoulders, Knees, and Toes/cabeza, hombros, piernas, pies*. Sydney, Aus.: Child's Play International.

Laden, Nina. 2000. *Peek-a-Who?* San Francisco: Chronicle Books.

Martin, Bill Jr., and Eric Carle. 1996. *Brown Bear, Brown Bear, What Do You See?* New York: Henry Holt and Company.

McDonald, Jill. 2020. *Construction Site*. Hello, World! series. New York: Doubleday Books for Young Readers.

Raffi. 2020. *Shake My Sillies Out.* New York: Knopf Books for Young Readers.

Smart, Camesha Monteith. 2021. *Finding Fun*. Pumpkin's Place.

## Transitioning to a New Class or School

Dewdney, Anna. 2009. *Llama Llama Misses Mama*. New York: Viking Books for Young Readers.

Gaiman, Neil. 2015. *Chu's First Day of School*. New York: Bloomsbury.

Henkes, Kevin. 2010. *Wemberly Worried*. New York: Greenwillow Books.

Olsen, Shannon. 2021. *A Letter from Your Teacher on the First Day of School*. Orange County, CA: Shannon Olsen.

Penfold, Alexandra. 2018. *All Are Welcome*. New York: Knopf.

Penn, Audrey. 2010. *The Kissing Hand*. Terre Haute, IN: Tanglewood.

## Trauma and Violence

Herman, Steve. 2019. *Help Your Dragon Cope with Trauma*. Tallahassee, FL: DG Books.

Holmes, Margaret M. 2000. *A Terrible Thing Happened*. Washington, DC: Magination Press.

# References and Recommended Reading

Ascher Shai, Tamar. 2011. "Taking a Stand: The Role of the Early Childhood Teacher in Educating against Homophobia." *Journal of Hate Studies* 9(1): 149–163.

BabySparks. 2017. "Crawling: A Key Step for Sensory-Motor Integration, Fine Motor Skills and Oral Motor Development." BabySparks. https://babysparks.com/2017/04/24/crawling-a-key-step-for-sensory-motor-integration-fine-motor-skills-oral-motor-development/#:~:text=Crawling%20builds%20fine%20motor%20skills,movements%20happen%20inside%20their%20mouths

Barnett, Melissa A., et al. 2020. "Influences of Parent Engagement in Early Childhood Education Centers and the Home on Kindergarten School Readiness." *Early Childhood Research Quarterly* 53(4): 260–273.

Bay Area Early Childhood Funders. 2007. *Play in the Early Years: Key to School Success: A Policy Brief.* El Cerrito, CA: Bay Area Early Childhood Funders.

Bayat, Mojdeh. 2011. "Clarifying Issues Regarding the Use of Praise with Young Children." *Topics in Early Childhood Special Education* 31(2): 121–128. doi: 10.1177/0271121410389339

Beasley, Elizabeth. 2020. "7 Serious Health Benefits of Laughter." Healthgrades. https://www.healthgrades.com/right-care/lifestyle-and-wellness/7-serious-health-benefits-of-laughter

Bell, Jennifer. 2020. "What Type of Lighting Should Be Used in Schools." Playground Professionals. https://playgroundprofessionals.com/play/school-and-education/what-type-lighting-should-be-used-schools

Bennett, Colette. 2019. "Stop Classroom Clutter: Think Before You Paint or Hang That Poster." ThoughtCo. https://www.thoughtco.com/decorating-your-classroom-4077035

Bergen, Doris. 2002. "The Role of Pretend Play in Children's Cognitive Development." *Early Childhood Research and Practice* 4(1). https://ecrp.illinois.edu/v4n1/bergen.html

Birbili, Maria. 2013. "Developing Young Children's Thinking Skills in Greek Early Childhood Classrooms: Curriculum and Practice." *Early Childhood Development and Care* 183(8): 1101–1114. doi: 10.1080/03004430.2013.772990

Blackmore, Annaliz. 2021. "What Is 'Midline' and Why Is 'Crossing the Midline'" Important for Your Child's Brain Development?" Centre of Movement. https://www.centreofmovement.com.au/what-is-midline-and-why-is-crossing-the-midline-important-for-your-childs-brain-development/

Bodrova, Elena, and Deborah J. Leong. 2003. "The Importance of Being Playful." *Educational Leadership* 60(7): 50–53.

Boston Children's Museum. 2013. *STEM Sprouts Teaching Guide*. Boston, MA: Boston Children's Museum. http://www.bostonchildrensmuseum.org/sites/default/files/pdfs/STEMGuide.pdf

Bulotsky-Shearer, Rebecca, Veronica Fernandez, Ximena Dominguez, and Heather L. Rouse. 2011. "Behavior Problems in Learning Activities and Social Interactions in Head Start Classrooms and Early Reading, Mathematics, and Approaches to Learning." *School Psychology Review* 40(1): 39–56.

Bush, Hillary H., Shana R. Cohen, Abbey S. Eisenhower, and Jan Blacher. 2017. "Parents' Educational Expectations for Young Children with Autism Spectrum Disorder." *Education and Training in Autism and Developmental Disabilities* 52(4): 357–368.

Byington, Teresa A., and YaeBin Kim. 2017. "Promoting Preschoolers' Emergent Writing." *Young Children* 72(5): 74–82.

Carlton, Elizabeth B. 2000. "Learning through Music: The Support of Brain Research." *Exchange* 22(5): 53–56.

Center on the Developing Child. n.d. "The Impact of Early Adversity on Children's Development." InBrief Series. Cambridge, MA: Harvard University, Center on the Developing Child. https://46y5eh11fhgw3ve3ytpwxt9r-wpengine.netdna-ssl.com/wp-content/uploads/2015/05/inbrief-adversity-1.pdf

Centers for Disease Control and Prevention. 2017. "Helping Young Children Thrive: Healthy Practices in the Early Care and Education

(LCL) Setting." https://www.cdc.gov/obesity/downloads/Early-Care-Education-ECE-WEB-508.pdf

Centers for Disease Control and Prevention. 2021. "How Much Physical Activity Do Children Need?" Centers for Disease Control and Prevention. https://www.cdc.gov/physicalactivity/basics/children/index.htm

Chang, Hedy, Deborah Stipek, and Nicolle Garza. 2006. *Deepening the Dialogue: Key Considerations for Expanding Access to High Quality Preschool in California.* Palo Alto, CA: Stanford University School of Education.

Chaudry, Ajay, and Heather Sandstrom. 2020. "Child Care and Early Education for Infants and Toddlers." *The Future of Children* 30(2): 165–190.

Cipani, Ennio. 1998. "Three Behavioral Functions of Classroom Noncompliance: Diagnostic and Treatment Implications." *Focus on Autism and Other Developmental Disabilities* 13(2): 66–72.

Cooklin, Amanda R., Rebecca Giallo, and Natalie Rose. 2011. "Parental Fatigue and Parenting Practices during Early Childhood: An Australian Community Survey." *Child: Care, Health and Development* 38(5): 654–664.

Dewar, Gwen. 2019. "Homework for Young Children: Is It Justified?" Parenting Science. https://www.parentingscience.com/homework-for-young-children.html

Dinkel, Danae, and Kailey Snyder. 2020. "Exploring Gender Differences in Infant Motor Development Related to Parent's Promotion of Play." *Infant Behavior and Development* 59 (May). https://doi.org/10.1016/j.infbeh.2020.101440

Duncan, Greg J., Jens Ludwig, and Katherine A. Magnuson. 2007. "Reducing Poverty through Preschool Interventions." *The Future of Children* 17(2): 143–160.

Dweck, Carol S. 2006. *Mindset: The New Psychology of Success.* New York: Random House.

Dweck, Carol S. 2007. "The Perils and Promises of Praise. The Wrong Kind of Praise Creates Self-Defeating Behavior. The Right Kind Motivates Students to Learn." *Educational Leadership* 65(2): 34–39.

Dweck, Carol S. 2008a. "Mindsets: How Praise Is Harming Youth and What Can Be Done about It." *School Library Media Activities Monthly* 24(5): 55–58.

Dweck, Carol S. 2008b. *Mindset: The New Psychology of Success.* Updated ed. New York: Ballantine Books.

Early Childhood STEM Working Group. 2017. *Early STEM Matters: Providing High-Quality STEM Experiences for All Young Learners.* Chicago: University of Chicago STEM Education and Erikson Institute. http://ecstem.uchicago.edu

Emerson, Andrea M., and Anna H. Hall. 2018. "Supporting Preschoolers' Writing Identities in the Scribbling Phase." *The Reading Teacher* 72(2): 257–260. doi:10.1002/trtr.169

Fisher, Anna V., Karrie E. Godwin, and Howard Seltman. 2014. "Visual Environment, Attention Allocation, and Learning in Young Children: When Too Much of a Good Thing May Be Bad." *Psychological Science* 25(7): 1362–1370. doi: 10.1177/0956797614533801

Gehris, Jeffrey S., et al. 2018. "Helping Your Child Develop Physical Literacy." *The Journal of Physical Education, Recreation and Dance* 89(6): 50–59.

Gilliam, Walter S. 2005. *Prekindergarteners Left Behind: Expulsion Rates in State Prekindergarten Systems.* FCD Policy Brief Number 3. New York: Foundation for Child Development.

Gilliam, Walter S., and Golan Shahar. 2006. "Preschool and Child Care Expulsion and Suspension: Rates and Predictors in One State." *Infants and Young Children* 19(3): 228–245.

Ginsburg, Kenneth R. 2007. "The Importance of Play in Promoting Healthy Child Development and Maintaining Strong Parent-Child Bonds." *Pediatrics* 119(1): 182–191.

*The Guardian.* 2020. "Who's a Clever Baby? How Speaking 'Parentese' Helps Your Baby Learn to Talk." *The Guardian*, February 4, https://www.theguardian.com/lifeandstyle/shortcuts/2020/feb/04/whosa-clever-baby-how-speaking-parentese-helps-your-baby-learn-to-talk

Haimovitz, Kyla, and Carol S. Dweck. 2017. "The Origins of Children's Growth and Fixed Mindsets: New Research and a New Proposal." *Child Development* 88(6): 1849–1859.

Hamre, Bridget K., and Robert C. Pianta. 2007. "Learning Opportunities in Preschool and Early Elementary Classrooms." In *School Readiness and the Transition to Kindergarten in the Era of Accountability*. Baltimore, MD: Paul H. Brookes.

Howes, Carollee, et al. 2008. "Ready to Learn? Children's Pre-Academic Achievement in Pre-Kindergarten Programs." *Early Childhood Research Quarterly* 23(1): 27–50.

Hyson, Marilou, and Jackie L. Taylor. 2011. "Caring about Caring: What Adults Can Do to Promote Young Children's Prosocial Skills." *Young Children* 66(3): 74–83.

Jaffe, Ken. n.d. "Why Early Childhood Programs Succeed, Why They Fail." International Child Resource Institute. https://www.icrichild.org/early-childhood-education-development

Jeon, Lieny, Cynthia K. Buettner, Ashley A. Grant, and Sarah N. Lang. 2019. "Early Childhood Teachers' Stress and Children's Social, Emotional, and Behavioral Functioning." *Journal of Applied Developmental Psychology* 61: 21–36.

Jones, Elizabeth. 2017. "A Meditation on Peacemaking." *Exchange* 39(6): 34–36.

Jung, Lee Ann. 2020. "There's More to Emotional Self-Regulation than Meets the Eye." *Educational Leadership* 78(3): 46–51.

Jung, Eunjoo, and Bora Jin. 2014. "Future Professionals' Perceptions of Play in Early Childhood Classrooms." *Journal of Research in Childhood Education* 28(3): 358–376. doi: 10.1080/02568543.2014.913277

Kid Sense. 2021. "Crossing the Body's Midline." Kid Sense. https://childdevelopment.com.au/areas-of-concern/fine-motor-skills/crossing-the-bodys-midline/

Kingston, Sharon, et al. 2013. "Parent Involvement in Education as a Moderator of Family and Neighborhood Socioeconomic Context on School Readiness among Young Children." *Journal of Community Psychology* 41(3): 265–276. doi: 10.1002/jcop.21528

Linder, Sandra M., and Angela Eckhoff. 2020. "Examples of STEAM." *Teaching Young Children* 13(3): 28–30.

Mashburn, Andrew J., et al. 2008. "Measures of Classroom Quality in Prekindergarten and Children's Development of Academic, Language, and Social Skills." *Child Development* 79(3): 732–749.

Matijević, Katarina, and Renata Bernić. 2020. "Is There a Connection between Reading to Children and the Child's Involvement in Reading Activities?" *Croatian Journal of Education* 22(3): 37–49.

Meece, Darrell, and Anne K. Soderman. 2010. "Setting the Stage for Young Children's Social Development." *Young Children* 65(4): 81–86.

Mills, Hannah. 2014. "The Importance of Creative Arts in Early Childhood Classrooms." *Texas Child Care Quarterly* 38(1).

Monahan, Kathryn C., Susan VanDerhei, Jordan Bechtold, and Elizabeth Cauffman. 2014. "From the School Yard to the Squad Car: School Discipline, Truancy, and Arrest." *Journal of Youth and Adolescence* 43(7): 1110–1122. https://doi.org/10.1007/s10964-014-0103-1

Myck-Wayne, Janice. 2010. "In Defense of Play: Beginning the Dialog about the Power of Play." *Young Exceptional Children* 13(4): 14–23. doi: 10.1177/1096250610376616

National Association for the Education of Young Children. 2009. "Developmentally Appropriate Practice in Early Childhood Programs Serving Children from Birth through Age 8." Position statement. Washington, DC: NAEYC. https://www.naeyc.org/sites/default/files/globally-shared/downloads/PDFs/resources/position-statements/PSDAP.pdf

Neale, Dave. 2020. "The Importance of Play in Early Childhood." *International Journal of Birth and Parent Education* 7(4): 10–12.

Norton, Amy. 2020. "Bringing the Forest to Kids' Daycare May Boost Young Immune Systems." Medical Xpress. https://medicalxpress. com/news/2020–10-forest-kids-daycare-boost- young. html#:~:text=Bringing%20the%20forest%20to%20kids%27%20 daycare%20may%20boost%20young%20immune%20systems,- by%20Amy%20Nortonandtext=Researchers%20in%20Finland%20 found%20that,to%20a%201ess%20inflammatory%20state

Omidvar, Nazanin, Tarah Wright, Karen Beazley, and Daniel Seguin. 2019. "Investigating Nature-Related Routines and Preschool Children's Affinity to Nature at Halifax Children's Centers." *The International Journal of Early Childhood Environmental Education* 6(2): 42–58.

Orrell-Valente, Joan, et al. 2007. "'Just Three More Bites': An Observational Analysis of Parents' Socialization of Children's Eating at Mealtime." *Appetite* 48(1): 37–45. doi: 10.1016/j. appet.2006.06.006

Parkes, Louise. 2015. "Giving STEM a Place in Early Childhood Classrooms." *Texas Child Care Quarterly* 39(3). http://www. childcarequarterly.com/pdf/winter15_stem.pdf

Pascoe, Elizabeth A., and Laura Smart Richman. 2009. "Perceived Discrimination and Health: A Meta-Analytic Review." *Psychological Bulletin* 135(4): 531–554.

Reiss, Albert J., and Jeffrey A. Roth. 2003. *Understanding and Preventing Violence*. Washington, DC: National Academies Press.

Richmond, Lindsey, and Michaela Marks. 2019. "Effect of Ability to Cross Midline on Performance of Handwriting." *Occupational Therapy Graduate Student Evidenced-Based Research Reviews* 39. https:// scholarworks.wmich.edu/ot_posters/39

Ritchhart, Ron, and David Perkins. 2008. "Making Thinking Visible." *Educational Leadership* 65(5): 57–61.

Ritz, Mariah, Amity Noltemeyer, Darrel Davis, and Jennifer Green. 2014. "Behavior Management in Preschool Classrooms: Insights Revealed through Systematic Observation and Interview." *Psychology in the Schools* 51(2): 181–197. doi: 10.1002/pits.21744

Roslund, Marja I., et al. 2020. "Biodiversity Intervention Enhances Immune Regulation and Health-Associated Commensal Microbiota among Daycare Children." *Science Advances* 6(42). doi: 10.1126/sciadv.aba2578

Schaack, Diana D., Vi-Nhuan Le, and Jennifer Stedron. 2020. "When Fulfillment Is Not Enough: Early Childhood Teacher Occupational Burnout and Turnover Intentions from a Job Demands and Resources Perspective." *Early Education and Development* 31(7): 1011–1030. doi: 10.1080/10409289.2020.1791648

Shonkoff, Jack, and Deborah Phillips, eds. 2000. *From Neurons to Neighborhoods: The Science of Early Childhood Development.* Washington, DC: National Academies Press.

Singer, Dorothy, G., Roberta Michnick Golinkoff, and Kathy Hirsh-Pasek, eds. 2006. *Play = Learning: How Play Motivates and Enhances Children's Cognitive and Social-Emotional Growth.* New York: Oxford University Press.

Suggate, Sebastian, Heidrun Stoeger, and Eva Pufke. 2017. "Relations between Playing Activities and Fine Motor Development." *Early Childhood Development and Care* 187(8): 1297–1310.

Trafton, Anne. 2018. "Back and Forth Exchanges Boost Children's Brain Response to tLanguage." MIT News. https://news.mit.edu/2018/conversation-boost-childrens-brain-response-language-0214

US Department of Education. 2016. *The State of Racial Diversity in the Educator Workforce.* Report. Washington, DC: US Department of Education. https://www2.ed.gov/rschstat/eval/highered/racial-diversity/state-racial-diversity-workforce.pdf

US Department of Health and Human Services (USDHHS) and Department of Education (DOE). 2014. *Policy Statement on Expulsion and Suspension Policies in Early Childhood Settings.* Washington, DC: USDHHS and DOE. https://www2.ed.gov/policy/gen/guid/school-discipline/policy-statement-ece-expulsions-suspensions.pdf

Venetsanou, Fotini, and Antonis Kambas. 2010. "Environmental Factors Affecting Preschoolers' Motor Development." *Early Childhood*

*Education Journal* 37(4): 319–327. doi: 10.1007/s10643–009–
0350-z

Virtual Lab School. n.d. "The Environment: Schedules and Routines."
Preschool Learning Environments. https://www.virtuallabschool.
org/preschool/learning-environments/lesson-5

Vitiello, Virginia E., D. Sarah Hadden, and Teachstone Policy Group.
2014. *Class System Implementation Guide: Aligned Improvement
Solutions*. Charlottesville, VA: Teachstone Training, LLC.

Warneken, Felix, and Michael Tomasello. 2006. "Altruistic Helping in
Human Infants and Young Chimpanzees." *Science* 311(5765): 1301–
1303. doi: 10.1126/science.1121448

Webster-Stratton, Carolyn. 1997. "Early Intervention for Families of
Preschool Children with Conduct Disorders." In *The Effectiveness of
Early Intervention*. Baltimore, MD: Brookes.

Wilkins, Arnold J. 2019. "Fluorescent Lighting in School Could Be
Harming Your Child's Health and Ability to Read." The Conversation.
https://theconversation.com/fluorescent-lighting-in-school-could-
be-harming-your-childs-health-and-ability-to-read-124330

Wymer, Sarah. C, Amanda P. Williford, and Ann S. L'hospital. 2020.
"Exclusionary Discipline Practices in Early Childhood." *Young
Children* 75(3): 36–44.

Zero to Three. 2016. "Learning to Write and Draw." Zero to Three.
https://www.zerotothree.org/resources/305-learning-to-write-and-
draw

Zhao, Li, Gail Heyman, Lulu Chen, and Kang Lee. 2017. "Praising Young
Children for Being Smart Promotes Cheating." *Psychological
Science* 28(2): 1868–1870. doi: 10.1177/09567 97617721529

Zhao, Li, et al. 2019. "Young Children Are More Likely to Cheat after
Overhearing that a Classmate Is Smart." *Developmental Science*
23(5): e12930. doi: 10.1111/desc.12930

# Index

## A

abilities, focus on, 44–45

alliteration, 86

antecedent-behavior-consequences (ABC). *See also* behavior/behavior management

observations and, 115, 119–120

use of, 112–113

art centers, 50. *See also* centers for play/learning

artistic expression. *See* creative expression

attention span

behavior and, 116, 120

child-friendly schedules and, 57–59

of toddlers, 36

authentic praise, 23

autonomy

child-friendly spaces and, 54–55

encouraging independence and, 52

## B

behavior/behavior management

about, 112–114

community of care and, 117–118

design and furnishings and, 48–50

ignoring behaviors, 116

interpretation and approach to behavior, 114–115

logical consequences and, 116–117, 120–121

observations and, 115, 119–120

positive behaviors and gratitude, recognizing and encouraging, 76

resources for, 118, 121, 140

sample letter about, 119–121

setting them up for success and, 115–116, 119–120

belly breaths, 4, 7

body awareness. *See also* physical development

emotions and, 78

physical development and, 100

self-regulation and, 98

building child-friendly schedules. *See* schedules

building on children's interests. *See* interests, building on

burnout, 3–4

## C

calming strategies, 78, 119, 120

centers for play/learning

child-friendly spaces and, 54

choice and, 43

design and furnishings for, 50

development, supporting with, 50–52

independent play and, 20

language and literacy and, 83

natural elements and, 108

power of play and, 14–15

changing your mind, 23–24

child-centered environments. *See also* environment; outdoor learning environments

    abilities, focus on, 44–45

    about, 41

    interests, starting with, 42

    involving children, 42–44, 46–47

    resources for, 45, 47, 140

    sample letter about, 46–47

child-friendly spaces

    about, 48

    design and furnishings for, 48–50

    independence and, 52

    learning centers and, 50–52

    resources for, 53

    sample letter about, 54–55

child-led exploration, 57, 62

children's books related to

    behavior, 140

    child-centered environments, 140

    diversity, 140–141

    fine motor development and writing, 142

    general encouragement, 142

    grief and loss, 142

    individuality and uniqueness of children, 141–142

    infants, 143–144

    intentional interactions and the power of yet, 143

    language and literacy, 144–145

    nurturing in nature, 145

    physical development, 145

    race and racism, 146

    safety, 146

    separation, 146

    social-emotional development, 147–148

    STEM for young children, 146–147

    toddlers, 148–149

    transitioning to a new class or school, 149

    trauma and violence, 149

choice

    child-centered environment and, 46

    individuality and uniqueness and, 61–65

    involving children, 42–44

chores

    child-centered environment and, 42–43, 46–47

    play and, 19

classroom displays, 124

collaboration

    diversity and, 68–69

    transitioning to a new class or school, 136–137

color and behavior, 49

communication

    behavior is communication, 112–121

    difficult situations and topics and, 129–130

    documenting the learning and, 127, 128

    language and literacy and, 81, 85

    parallel talk, 36

    parentese, 32

transitioning to a new class or school and, 136

community helpers, 68, 71

community of care, 117–118

construction centers, 50. *See also* centers for play/learning

COVID-19 pandemic
    difficult situations and topics and, 130, 134
    learning centers and, 52
    needs and roles as teachers and, vi
    relationships and, 3
    schedules and, 56

creating a child-centered environment where children thrive. *See* child-centered environments

creative expression
    individuality and uniqueness and, 61, 64
    physical development and, 97–98
    play and, 16–17

critical thinking and problem solving, 103–104

curriculum
    interest, starting with, 42
    and understanding the power of play, 13, 14

**D**

dancing/dance
    calming strategies and, 78, 119
    creative expression and, 16
    exercise, 4, 7, 96
    physical development and, 100

toddlers and, 36, 39

death, 129. *See also* difficult situations and topics

design and furnishings, behavior and, 48–50

development
    developmental checklists, 124–125
    developmental disabilities, 66
    diversity, 66
    social-emotional development, 72–79

difficult situations and topics
    about, 129
    behavior and, 113
    communicating with families, 129–130
    death, 129
    grief and loss, 130, 131, 142
    honesty, 130
    learning together in a safe space, 131–132
    reflecting on, 130
    resources for, 132–133, 142
    sample letter about, 134–135

discipline. *See* behavior/behavior management

discovery centers, 108. *See also* centers for play/learning

diversity
    about, 66–68
    collaboration and, 68–69
    community connections and, 69
    diverse themes, 68
    resources for, 69–70, 140–141

sample letter about, 71

documenting the learning

    about, 122

    formative assessments, 124–125

    notes, photos, and videos, 123

    observing and, 122–125

    resources for, 125–126

    sample letter about, 127–128

dramatic play, 73

dramatic play centers, 50–51, 54. *See also* centers for play/learning

**E**

eating habits, 98, 100–101

effort

    documenting the learning and, 128

    growth mindset and, 22, 23

embracing and celebrating our diverse and beautiful world. *See* diversity

emergent learning/curriculum, 15, 42

emotions

    body awareness, 78

    difficult situations and topics, 135

    exploring emotions, 73–74

    learning together in a safe space, 131–132

empathy, 74–75

encouraging children's individuality and uniqueness. *See* individuality and uniqueness of children

engineering, 103. *See also* STEM for young children

environment

    behavior management and, 119

child-centered environments. *See* child-centered environments

child-friendly spaces and, 48–55

independence and, 52

for infants, 28

outdoor learning environments. *See* outdoor learning environments

setting them up for success and, 115–116

social-emotional development and, 72

"yes" environments, 40

errands, 7, 19, 110

exercise, 4, 7, 20, 96

expectations

    behavior management and, 116, 117, 120

    transitioning to a new class or school and, 137

expulsion rates, 114–115

**F**

families

    diversity and, 69

    transitioning to a new class or school, 137

fine motor development and writing

    about, 88

    resources for, 91–92, 142

    sample letter about, 93–95

    strengthening little fingers and, 89–91, 93–94

    writing for authentic purpose and, 88–89

fingerplays, 91, 94

fixed mindset, 22

formative assessments, 124–125

free play, 14–15, 107

**G**

general encouragement, children's books related to, 142. *See also* individuality and uniqueness of children

gratitude, 5, 8, 76

grief and loss

difficult situations and topics, 130, 131

resources for, 142

group activities, 36, 50, 57

growth mindset

intentional interactions and the power of yet and, 21–24

sample letter about, 25–26

**H**

handling difficult situations and topics with care. *See* difficult situations and topics

hand washing, 51, 52

home learning activities, 9

how can I tell if they're learning. *See* documenting the learning

how to use this book, 1–2

hyperactivity, 49

**I**

illnesses, 129. *See also* difficult situations and topics

independent play, 20

individuality and uniqueness of children

about, 61

child-led exploration and, 62

resources for, 65, 141–142

respecting individuality, 62–63

sample letter about, 64–65

infants

about, 27

observing and planning for, 27–29

resources for, 30–31, 34, 143–144

routines and, 29–30

sample letter about, 32–33

simple activities for, 29

supporting parents of, 30

instruction

attention span and, 57

behavior management and, 116, 120

teacher-directed instruction, 13

intentional interactions and the power of yet

about, 21–24

growth mindset and, 21–24

resources for, 24, 143

sample letter about, 25–26

intentions, 64

interests, building on

activities and, 15–16

child-initiated activities and interests, 13, 19, 42

introduction, 1–2

involving infants. *See* infants

**L**

language and literacy

about, 80

exploring emotions and, 73–74

infants and, 28, 32

playing with children, 81–83

reading and, 80–81, 87

resources for, 83–84, 87, 144–145

sample letter about, 85–87

talking, 81

toddlers and, 39, 40

writing and, 83, 86–87

laughter, 5, 8

letter recognition, 52, 80–81, 82

library centers, 50, 54. *See also* centers for play/learning

lighting, 48–49

listening

behavior and, 112

child-centered environment and, 46

learning together in a safe space and, 131

loose parts, 51

**M**

manipulatives and STEM, 104

manipulatives centers, 50, 51. *See also* centers for play/learning

mathematics, 103. *See also* STEM for young children

mental health, 96

midline, crossing, 97

minibreaks, 4, 7

motivation, 22

music. *See* singing/songs

**N**

napping, 101

National Association for the Education of Young Children (NAEYC), 21

nature walks, 108

no, use of, 44

nurturing in nature

about, 107–109

resources for, 109, 145

sample letter about, 110–111

**O**

observations

and behavior, 112, 115

and documenting the learning, 122–125

and planning for infants, 27–29

open-ended questions

documenting the learning and, 123

intentional interactions and the power of yet and, 24, 26

language and literacy and, 87

STEM for young children and, 106

opening, closing, and clipping skills, 90–91, 94

outdoor learning environments. *See also* child-centered environments; environment

attention span and, 57

child-friendly spaces and, 48

learning centers and, 52

nurturing in nature and, 107–111

physical development and, 96–97

**P**

parallel talk, 36

parentese, 32

parents

about, 9

parent mixers, 11

parent night, 10–11

play-based learning and, 13

sample letter about, 12

supporting parents, 5–6, 30

teacher-parent relationships, vi

use of term, 1

partnering with parents. *See* parents

phonological awareness, 80–81, 82, 86

physical aggression, 113

physical development

about, 96

creative expression and, 97–98

crossing the midline, 97

eating habits and, 98, 100–101

movement and, 96

outdoor play and, 96–97

reading and, 98

resources for, 99, 145

sample letter about, 100–101

physical movement. *See* exercise

planning for specific needs and interests

for infants, 27–29

for toddlers, 35

play

about, 13–14

building on children's interests and, 15–16

centers for play. *See* centers for play/learning

creative expression and, 16–17

importance of, 9, 14

infants and, 33

making time for, 15

outdoor play, 96–97

physical development and, 100

playing with children, 16, 36–37, 81–83, 127–128

resources for, 17–18

sample letter about, 19–20

toddlers and, 39

play-based learning, vi, 10–11, 13

playdough, use of, 90

portfolios, 123–124

positive behaviors, 76, 79. *See also* behavior/behavior management

power of yet. *See* intentional interactions and the power of yet

praise, 22–23

pretend-play area. *See* dramatic play centers

problem solving

critical thinking and, 103–104

growth mindset and, 22

social-emotional development and, 75

supporting each child's unique needs and, 76

process quality, 41

**Q**

quitting, use of term, 23

**R**

race and racism

    demonstrating respect and, 129

    discrimination, 113, 134, 135

    diversity, 66, 71

    leading by example and, 134

    resources for, 146

reading. *See also* language and literacy

    child-friendly spaces and, 49, 50

    difficult situations and topics and, 135

    diversity and, 68

    encouraging individuality and uniqueness and, 64

    infants and, 32, 33

    intentional interactions and the power of yet and, 25

    phonological awareness and, 82

    physical development and, 98

    schedules and, 56, 59

    social-emotional development and, 73, 79

    STEM for young children and, 102, 103

    toddlers and, 36, 39

redirection, 40, 116

Reggio Emilia, 42, 61

relationships

    community of care and, 117–118

    documenting the learning and, 125

    intentional interactions and the power of yet and, 21

    self-care and, 3

    social-emotional development and, 72

    teacher-parent relationships, vi

    teacher-student relationships, vi

rest routines, 101

rhymes, 80, 82, 86

role models

    difficult situations and topics and, 130

    empathy and, 74

    physical development and, 101

    positive behaviors and gratitude and, 76

    social-emotional development and, 79

role-playing

    exploring emotions and, 73

    supporting social-emotional development and, 79

routines

    choice and, 64

    infants and, 28, 29–30, 32

    rest and, 101

    schedules and, 56

    self-care and, 7–8

    toddlers and, 37

    transitioning to a new class or school and, 138

**S**

safety

    difficult situations and topics and, 132

    needs for, 114

    resources for, 146

schedules

about, 56

attention span and, 57–59

example of, 57–58

infants and, 29–30

involving children with, 43

resources for, 59

routines and, 56–57

sample letter about, 60

setting them up for success and, 115–116

time for play and, 15

transitions and, 58–59

visual schedules, 56–57

science, 102. *See also* STEM for young children

self-care

about, 3–4

breathing deeply and getting moving and, 4, 7

gratitude and support and, 5, 8

laughter and, 5, 8

parents, supporting, 5–6

resources for, 6, 8

sample letter about, 7–8

self-confidence

abilities, focus on, 44–45

respecting children's individuality and, 63

self-help skills, 90, 93

self-regulation

body awareness and, 78, 98

developing, 39

social-emotional development, 72–73

self-talk, 36

sensory play

fine motor development and writing and, 91, 94

learning centers and, 50, 54

outdoor learning environment and, 108

simple activities for infants and, 29

separation

difficult situations and topics, 129, 131, 134

resources for, 146

setting up child-friendly spaces. *See* child-friendly spaces

shaky sounds, 29

singing/songs

calming strategies and, 78

creative expression and, 17, 64, 97

fingerplays and, 91, 93

hand washing and, 52

infants and, 33

routines and, 58

toddlers and, 39

Sinkkonen, Aki, 107

social-emotional development

about, 72–73

empathy, 74–75

exploring emotions, 73–74

infants and, 28

positive behaviors and gratitude and, 76

problem solving and conflict management and, 75

resources for, 76–77, 147–148

sample letter about, 78–79

supporting unique needs and, 75–76

solitary play, 50

sorry, use of, 75

STEM for young children

about, 102–103

critical thinking and problem solving and, 103–104

manipulating materials and, 104

resources for, 105, 146–147

sample letter about, 106

strengthening little fingers, 89–91

stress balls, use of, 90, 93

support

behavior issues and, 121

child-centered environment and, 46

for parents, 5–6

self-care and, 5, 8

T

teacher-child interactions. *See also* intentional interactions and the power of yet

fine motor development and writing and, 88

impact on development and learning and, 21

infants and, 27, 28

language and literacy and, 80

process quality and, 41

teacher-directed instruction, 13, 57

teachers

burnout, 3–4

relationship with parents, vi

role modeling, 74, 79, 79, 101, 130

teacher-parent relationships, 5–6

use of term, 1

tearing and cutting, 90, 94

technology, 103. *See also* STEM for young children

terrific toddlers. *See* toddlers

themes

child-centered environment and, 43

diverse themes, 68

encouraging individuality and uniqueness and, 62

toddlers

about, 35

and encouraging exploration, 36

planning for specific needs and interests of, 35

playing with children, 36–37

resources for, 37–38, 148–149

and roles and routines, 37

sample letter about, 39–40

transitioning to a new class or school

about, 136

and collaborating with colleagues, 136–137

and collaborating with families, 137

resources for, 149

sample letter about, 138–139

and talking about it, 136

transitions

behavior management and, 119

movement and, 96

schedules and, 58–59

trauma and violence

    behavior and, 114, 121

    difficult situations and topics, 129, 134, 135

    resources for, 149

**V**

vocabulary, 24. *See also* language and literacy

**W**

welcome letter, vi–vii

word games, 85–86

writing. *See also* fine motor development and writing

    writing centers, 50, 83. *See also* centers for play/learning

    writing for authentic purpose, 88–89

    writing in the air, 86–87

**Y**

yes, use of, 44

"yes" environments, 40

yet, power of. *See* intentional interactions and the power of yet